Central Park Memories

Central Park Memories

The Breedon Books
Publishing Company
Derby

First published in Great Britain by
The Breedon Books Publishing Company Limited
Breedon House, 44 Friar Gate, Derby, DE1 1DA.
1999

ISBN 1 85983 180 X

Printed and bound by Butler & Tanner Ltd., Selwood Printing Works,
Caxton Road, Frome, Somerset.

Colour separations and jacket printing by GreenShires Ltd, Leicester.

Contents

Acknowledgements

Getting together a large collection of photographs that – for the most part – were taken at Central Park was no easy task. There are plenty of great photographs of Challenge Cup Finals at Wembley and of other Cup Finals involving Wigan at 'neutral' grounds – but they are part of the Wigan Rugby League story, rather than the Central Park story. Outside help was greatly appreciated and, as it turned out, vital.

For pictures, thanks go to Harold Farrimond, John Leatherbarrow, Nick Fairhurst, Paul Simpson, Gary Brunskill, Gerald Webster, Frank Orrell, Graham Gerrard whose father Tom took many great photographs and films at Central Park, Len Hudson at Wigan Heritage Service, Neil Cain, David Duckworth, Philip Harris, Kevin Sullivan and John Ryding. Lucy and Megan Bradshaw helped me with their photographs of their illustrious grandfather Tom. I have also received plenty of assistance from John Oakes at Micron Video, Jim and Frank Bretherton and Jack Forshaw. John Martin provided photographs of past days at The Riverside Club. Kevin Johnson kindly gave me access to his amazing collection of old programmes, tickets and fixture cards, and Carolyn Evans was also very helpful.

For the 'bricks and mortar' history of Central Park, David Bithell was a great help – his knowledge of the ground is literally encyclopaedic. Brian Murphy also lent great assistance. Other anecdotes have been extracted from past copies of the *Wigan Observer*, and thanks must go to all those interviewed whose own experiences and achievements at Central Park are, after all, what made the ground so special.

The following books were also consulted
The Best Years of Our Lives – Paul Wilson
The Rugby League Challenge Cup – An Illustrated History – Les Hoole
The Illustrated History of Wigan RLFC – Jack Winstanley
An Illustrated History of Wigan v Saints Derby Matches – Robert Gate
Wigan RLFC 1895-1986 – Ian Morrison

Introduction

One of the most famous landmarks in rugby league. The pavilion building before it disappeared beneath the metal cladding of the Whitbread Stand in 1991.

WIGAN town centre does not have a familiar landmark. There is nothing at the hub of this great industrial town that sets it apart from from, say, the likes of Bolton, or Blackburn. It is a Lancashire town. But there is just one building on the edge of the town centre that, as soon as you see it, you know you are in Wigan. You can be nowhere else in the world. And they have just pulled it down.

John Prescott, a committee member of the club in 1902 when Wigan first found a true home for itself, wanted Central Park to become such a landmark. It

achieved that status in a short space of time – the first ever New Zealand touring team would play there before World War One and in 1950 club officials were talking of developing the ground further to hold an incredible 70,000 people.

The fortunes of rugby league dipped, from the glory years of the 1940s, 1950s and 1960s, and such grandiose plans ultimately never made it off the drawing board. New safety laws and the constraints of the site itself meant the development of such a huge stadium would always be unlikely, if not impossible.

But the magic of Central Park has little to do with its structure. It has little to do with the old pavilion building, a landmark within a landmark in rugby league. Central Park was all about the great teams that played there and enormous gatherings of supporters that would pack the terraces. The people made the place.

Central Park will be remembered as a ground that was part of the community. In its early years it was surrounded by houses – many people would walk to the ground, youngsters would hop over garden fences. It was close to the railway station and many supporters who

View of Central Park from the air.

lived further away made their pilgrimage first by rail and then by foot.

Central Park will be remembered for hosting some of the greatest games the sport has seen. The pitch has been graced by every big name in rugby league – those in cherry and white hoops, those of the opposition, and international stars in their touring sides.

Most of all, Central Park will be remembered as the home of rugby league. It symbolised the sport and success within it the world over. No other ground came close.

Wigan has a new landmark now. A modern stadium, with symmetric curves and gleaming metal. It dwarfs everything in Wigan, and everything we have ever seen in the town.

But for now, and perhaps for a long time to come, when people think of Wigan Rugby League Club they will think of only one ground.

Here are 97 years of memories to explain why.

Under the rainbow:
There may have been no pot of gold at Central Park but there was plenty of silverware. This photograph was taken from one of the highrise flats in Scholes.

The Central Park Story

The Days Before Central Park

RUGBY was played in Wigan long before Central Park existed but the roots of the league code only emerged some seven years before a ball was kicked at the ground. Wigan FC, as it was first known, was formed by members of Wigan Cricket Club at a meeting in the Royal Hotel in Standishgate in November 1872.

Home games were played off Upper Dicconson Street at Folly Field. Four years later the club merged with Up Holland FC to form the Wigan and District Football Club, and home games were played at the cricket ground in Prescott Street. Yet within 18 months the club folded.

Another rugby club called Wigan Wasps was formed in 1879 after a meeting at the Dicconson Arms, and they played at a ground in Upper Dicconson Street. Blue and white jerseys became cherry and white by 1886 when the club was known as Wigan Football Club, and it moved back to Prescott Street when the cricket club relocated to Bull Hey.

Based from Prescott Street, the club became the founder members of the Northern Union after the Rugby Union breakaway in 1895. In 1901 the Prescott Street land was needed by the railway and Wigan was forced to move temporarily to Springfield Park, then used as an athletics and cycling track and home to Wigan United Football Club. Rugby matches had to fit around the football programme and rent increases meant the club had to look elsewhere once again.

On January 23rd 1902 a meeting was held at the Public Hall in King Street when it was decided to negotiate for the lease of a new ground already being used by pub rugby teams, nicknamed Joe Hill's field after a butcher of the same name had used it for grazing. The land, off Powell Street, was offered by the Great Central Railway company under a long-term lease. Previously travelling fairs and circuses had used the land but the railway company bought it with a view to laying a track from Wigan to Blackpool. That never happened, so councillor and rugby club committee member John Prescott, whose house – Hill Cottage – overlooked the plot of land, had the idea that Wigan could build their own home there.

Throughout 1902 the committee, having raised £1,000, prepared Joe Hill's field as a rugby ground and Central Park – as it became known – hosted its first ever game of rugby league on September 6th 1902, against Batley. Wigan won 14-8, and right winger Jimmy Barr had the honour of scoring the first-ever try there. A crowd of between 8,000 and 10,000 saw the game in glorious, sunny weather – a fitting start to Central Park's 97 years.

WIGAN FOOTBALL CLUB.—The first match of the above club will be played on Saturday afternoon next, in the Folly-field, Upper Dicconson-street, Wigan. The prospects of the club are exceedingly encouraging; the Mayor has kindly consented to act as president, already upwards of 50 members have been enrolled, and the promptitude with which the preliminary arrangements have been carried out promises well for the future success of the movement. It is expected that matches will be arranged with the clubs of several neighbouring towns during the season.

This notice appeared in the *Wigan Observer* on November 29th 1872, signalling the birth of Wigan Rugby League.

Foundations

AT FIRST players had to change at the Prince of Wales pub in

Wigan 14 Batley 8
September 6th 1902

THE first ever game at Central Park. Batley were known as the Gallant Youths and were the holders of the Northern Union Cup for three years out of the first five of its inception.

A total of 10,000 spectators went to the game and saw a good home win – and they only had to wait three minutes to see the first of many tries to be scored there.

Right winger Jimmy Barr touched down in the corner and the score was converted by Rothwell. Wigan's attacking play was excellent but the Batley players defended their line well.

Then Davies and Wilson were caught fumbling the ball and Rouse took advantage to grab the ball and score to give Wigan an 8-0 lead.

Davies reduced that advantage with a try which he converted himself, but Halliwell scored for the home side before the interval.

In the second half Halliwell scored again, and Wolstenholme touched down for the visitors to bring up the final score. Wigan backs Barr, Rouse and Eckersley were injured in the match.

The teams on that historic first day were:

Wigan: Mason, Barr, Eckersley, MacAuley, Rouse, Nelson, Rothwell, Ball, Brown, Hilton, Halliwell, Collier, Vickers, Barton, Beezley.

Batley: Wilson, Davies, Fitzgerald, Goodall, Kershaw, Oakland, Midgley, Rogers, Stubler, Munns, Fizzard, Wolstenholme, Dewes, Mozler, Judge. The referee was Mr Marshall from Bradford.

Total gate receipts for the first season at Central Park were £3,092 – but it was not so successful on the pitch and Wigan finished 16th in the table.

Greenough Street because there were no changing rooms at the ground, while crowds stood on banks of colliery spoil on what is now called the Popular Side. A wooden Douglas Stand was built some years later and provided seating for around 2,000 people, as well as press accommodation.

In their first season at Central Park, Wigan won 10, lost 18 and drew six, and attracted attendances of more than 10,000 for games against Leigh, Swinton, Halifax, Hull and Broughton Rangers. In the second season, Wigan won 11, lost 17 and drew six and finished 10th in the table, but they won the West Lancashire Cup.

In the 1905-06 season Wigan became the first winners of the Lancashire Cup.

By 1907 the Popular side was partially terraced and the Douglas

One of the earliest team photographs to be taken at Central Park. This 1904-05 team were the winners of the West Lancashire Cup.

Stand lengthened. On November 3rd that year 30,000 fans saw Wigan winger Jim Leytham score a hat-trick as the club beat New Zealand 12-8. There was drama before the game even started. A section of fencing around the pitch collapsed under the weight of the

spectators but thankfully no one was hurt. After the tour ended Lance Todd, the Kiwi centre, signed for Wigan and made his debut against Oldham on February 19th 1908 in front of a midweek crowd of 20,000. Unfortunately, Oldham won 7-3.

Another pre-First World War line-up. Back row (left to right): Battersby, Thomas, Blears, Brooks, Ramsdale, Leytham, Jenkins. Front: Silcock, Cheetham, Price (captain), Sharrock, Trehorne, Barton.

On January 30th 1909 more than 30,000 fans watched Wigan beat Oldham 23-10. It was a top of the table clash, gate receipts totalled £672 from the record league attendance, and applica-tions for seats had, according to the *Wigan Observer* and *District Advertiser*, 'poured in from all parts of the country'. At the end of the season Wigan beat Oldham 7-3 at Salford in the championship play-off to win the league, and Central Park staged a fireworks and brass band party to celebrate their sea-son.

The previous season's improve-ment works on the ground had

Wigan in 1908. Back row (left to right): G. Rigby (assistant trainer), Silcock, Ramsdale, Johnston, Blears, Cheetham, Whittaker, J. Hesketh (trainer). Front: Gleave, Jenkins, Todd, Leytham, Sharrock, Miller, Thomas.

Wigan 12 New Zealand 8
November 9th 1907

THIS was the first ever game featuring rugby league tourists New Zealand, and a record 25,000 people went along to Central Park to see the match.

Both sides went into the game with great winning records, so something had to give. Jimmy Leytham scored a hat-trick for Wigan – his first touchdown came after five minutes, but the visitors hit back with great forward play and a try from Wrigley.

Lance Todd, who joined Wigan after the tour was over, came close to giving the visitors the lead before skipper Leytham grabbed his second try.

He got the third with a great run in the second half, Jenkins increased Wigan's lead, and New Zealand only came back into the game later on when Cross scored.

Wigan played some of their best rugby and were the first side to beat the touring team.

Wigan: Sharrock, Leytham, Jenkins, T. Thomas, Miller, Battersby, J. Thomas, Cheetham, Silcock, Blears, Ramsdale, Brooks, Wilcock
New Zealand: Turtill, Wrigley, Row, Messenger, Smith, Todd, Wynyard, Lile, Pearce, Cross, Wright, Byrne, Tyler.

Jimmy Leytham, who scored a hat-trick against New Zealand in 1907. In all he scored 258 tries and kicked 267 goals in his 280 Wigan appearances between 1903 and 1911.

cost the club £774 11s 6d, but changes did not stop there. In May 1909 work started on a pavilion which would provide players' baths and changing rooms, gym, office accommodation and a committee room. The two-storey building was completed in four months! What would become one of the most

1908-09, Wigan RL Team and Committee with trophies. Back row (left to right): Hargreaves, Wood, Bouchier (vice-chairman), Laing, Counsell, Prescott, Dr Monks (hon. surgeon). Middle: Latham (treasurer), Taylor (secretary), Brown, Whittaker, Barton, Francis, Johnston, Ramsdale, Blears, Cheetham, Henderson, Hesketh (trainer). Sitting: Jones, Prescott, Gleave, Miller, Todd (vice-captain), Counsell (chairman), Leytham (captain), Jenkins, Sharrock, Thomas.

Wigan became the first team to beat the Australians during their 1911-1912 tour of Great Britain, winning the game 7-2 on October 28th 1911 at Central Park. Aussie skipper McKivatt is about to feed the scrum, while Wigan stand-off Johnny Thomas is on the extreme left and Jimmy Sharrock, Wigan's full-back, stands in the foreground.

famous landmarks in the rugby league world was opened on September 4th 1909 and had cost £1,246 7s 11d to build.

In 1909 the lease of the land from the Great Central Railway company was due to expire, but Wigan extended it further by 14 years as they confirmed their desire to stay at Central Park. Proposals to float the club in that year's annual general meeting, however, were turned down with a large majority of votes.

Oldham's visit to Central Park on January 8th 1910 attracted another record crowd, now housed in a Douglas Stand that extended beyond the dead ball lines and a Spion Kop which had a wooden cover.

In the summer of 1910 the ground was being used as a venue for wrestling matches, attracting crowds of up to 4,000. One bout, between Bolton's Tom Rose and Jack 'Whistler' Carroll of Hindley went on for nearly four hours without deciding a winner. Carroll eventually agreed to retire!

In October 1910 a new scoreboard was used for the first time, and the following year a cover was built for the Popular Side, which became known as the Dutch Barn. Built in two parts, it was 80 feet long and its roof was distinctive. The front half was rounded while the rear was pitched, and it became wider towards the Spion Kop end. Very often spectators would risk life and limb by climbing onto the roof to get a better view of the action!

Australia met Wigan on October 28th 1911 for the third time, and Wigan once again got the better of them, winning 7-2 in front of a 25,000 crowd.

The Kangaroos had been unbeaten on their tour until then, and the game made newspaper headlines.

In 1910 through to 1913 Wigan

George Formby's dad gets to kick-off a game at Central Park on December 7th 1912. Wigan beat Hunslet 22-13.

were beaten championship play-off finalists but would not reach the Final again until 1922 – when they won it. Despite the league disappointments they won the Lancashire Cup in 1912.

The 1913-14 rugby team with the Lancashire Cup. Back row (left to right): W. Counsell (committee), Wood (vice-chairman), Cllr Walkden (committee). Third row: Francis, Seeling (vice-captain), Ramsdale, Ald. Dickinson (Mayor), Coldrick, Williams, Laing. Second row: Prescott (committee), Cllr J. Counsell (chairman), Todd, Sharrock (captain), Jenkins, Silcock, Henderson (president). Front row: Bradley, Thomas, Walford, Gleave.

In 1913 Wigan played Huddersfield in the Challenge Cup and although the home side lost 14-5, Central Park was swelled with a record 33,000 fans. Towards the end of the season a small raised gallery was built at the rear of the Popular Side, and by this time even the A-team matches were attracting 5,000 supporters.

The club was going from strength to strength by then but the advent of World War One would put the game on hold.

World War One

THE Northern Union continued through the war but the sport was depleted as many players and supporters were enlisted. In October 1914 the Field Artillery, training at Winstanley Park, were invited to Central Park where they saw Wigan beat Hull. As the 1914-15 season went on, attendances fell, despite the club dropping its admission prices. But by the end of the year 10 Wigan players were involved in the war and club membership dropped from 1,400 to 709.

The Northern Union suspended competitive rugby in the summer of 1915 and all that remained were a few unofficial leagues and friendly matches. In September that year Central Park was used for a recruitment parade and the drill work all but ruined the pitch for a forthcoming friendly against Oldham.

In 1918 finances were so stretched at Central Park that the club used a timber shortage to its advantage and sold the Spion Kop cover for £452. The club made a loss four years in a row and annu-

al general meetings, which were previously held in the 2,000-capacity Queens Hall, could now be staged in the Central Park pavilion.

In January 1919 the county games resumed and the Northern Union, which a month later lifted the ban on professionalism, hoped to restart normal league action the following year.

During the war the ground had fallen into a poor state, and in the 1919-1920 season a lot of money was spent on repairs. Even broken goal posts had to be replaced. Local timber merchants John Heaton and Sons came to the rescue and erected posts in August 1919 that were 60ft high and described as the 'finest in the county'.

As normal service was resumed, so the crowds began to return and Wigan were about to enter a boom period for the sport.

The Sullivan Era

A RECORD 33,347 people watched Wigan beat Huddersfield 12-8 on March 3rd 1920 when the Fartowners made their first post-war trip to Central Park. It helped put the club in profit for the year and more repairs were carried out in the close season, stands and rails were painted and the pitch treated to provide better playing surface.

Even so, the terracing was still pit dirt held in timber troughs, and crush barriers were horizontal strips of wood supported by railway sleepers, and were scattered about the terraces in no particular order.

The following year the Great Central Railway sought to dispose of the land on which the ground was built, declaring it surplus to requirements. The club's committee met and agreed that the club should become a limited company,

Jim Sullivan kicking for goal at Central Park.

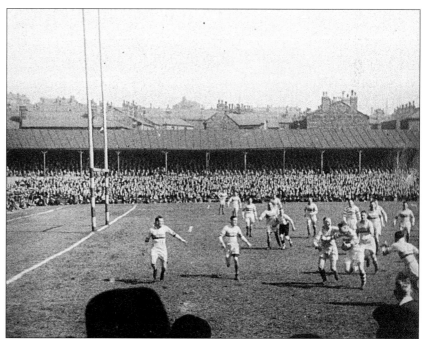
A rare photograph showing Jim Sullivan in action, handing-off the defender as he charges for the try-line.

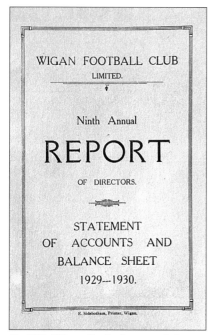

By 1921 Wigan Rugby League club was registered as a limited company. They were Wigan Football Club Ltd, and as a business the club now had shareholders to satisfy.

WIGAN FOOTBALL CLUB
LIMITED.

Ninth Annual

REPORT

OF DIRECTORS.

STATEMENT OF ACCOUNTS AND BALANCE SHEET
1929—1930.

E. Sidebotham, Printer, Wigan.

enabling it to buy the land outright. Excluding chief rent, it cost £500.

Wigan Football Club Ltd was registered on May 12th 1921 and the capital was £16,000 made up of £1 shares. Members could buy blocks of eight shares and directors, of which there would be no more than 10, would hold 48 shares. Finally, the club owned Central Park.

The club received another sig-

nificant boost in 1921. Jim Sullivan arrived at Central Park on June 18th as a 17-year-old and devoted the remaining 56 years of his life to the town of Wigan.

He could have played international rugby union for Wales, his home country, but chose to move to the North. He was signed from Cardiff Rugby Union and announced his arrival in rugby league by posting the season's top score of 100 goals. He was in the

Jim Sullivan.

before becoming an annual event from 1959 onwards.

In 1924 Wigan were back at Broughton in the championship play-off, but lost to Batley 13-7 in front of a disappointing 13,729 crowd. But at Rochdale Wigan won the Challenge Cup for the first time in their history, beating Oldham 21-4.

The Central Park programme from Wigan v Huddersfield, February 23rd 1924. Wigan won the game 27-8.

18-strong squad that won the 1921-22 championship, Wigan beating Oldham 13-2 at Broughton in the Final.

Jerry Shea was the solitary try scorer and Sullivan kicked four goals, with Tommy Howley adding a fifth. Wigan also won the Lancashire Cup in 1922, beating Leigh 20-2 at Salford.

The first seven-a-side tournament was hosted at Central Park on May 5th 1923, as well as a players' 100 yards sprint handicap. A disappointing 1,000 crowd watched Wigan beat Barrow 18-10 in the sevens final, and the event was not staged again until 1949

Wigan with the Northern Union League Championship Cup in 1921-22. It was the first piece of silverware the club won in Jim Sullivan's era, here shown at the back, third from left.

Wigan 21 Widnes 0
August 27th 1921

Jim Sullivan, whose record of 2,867 goals between 1921-22 and 1945-46 could prove impossible to beat. Sullivan kicked 100 goals every season until the war-interrupted 1939-40 year. He made 774 appearances for Wigan and played in 921 games in all, scoring 4,883 points for his club and more than 6,000 in total. He toured Australia and made World War Two appearances for Bradford Northern, Dewsbury and Keighley. He was player-coach at Central Park from 1932 but in 1946 he concentrated solely on coaching and guided the club through one of its most successful eras.

WIGAN had signed some Welsh players after a poor season and this campaign opener was notable for the debut of 17-year-old full-back Jim Sullivan.

He scored five goals from six attempts that day, and the rest, as they say, is history. He had a cool head, good judgement and, of course, he was a great goal-kicker.

He opened the scoring and Coldrick and Coles added tries to put Wigan well ahead by the break. Sullivan kicked two penalties and Jerram added a drop goal to take Wigan further ahead in the second half.

Hesketh scored a further try and Sullivan ended the game as he had started, kicking a goal. He was named Man of the Match, and Wigan had unearthed a legend.

Wigan: Sullivan, Coles, Howley, Hurcombe, Llewellyn, Hesketh, Jerram, Hodder, Roffey, Woods, Banks, Coldrick, Shaw.

Widnes: Brassington, Gregory, Redmond, Taylor, Stockley, Kelly, O'Gara, Townsend, Corcoran, J. Higgins, Reid, Johnson, T. Higgins.

Wigan		Huddersfield	
Full-Back	1 Sullivan	Full-Back	1 Oliver
Three-Qrs	2 Ring	Three-Qrs	2 May
	3 Howley		3 Howarth
	4 Parker		4 McTighe
	5 Van Heerden		5 Watts
Half-Backs	6 Jerram	Half-Backs	6 Rogers
	7 Hurcombe		7 Williams
Forwards	8 Webster	Forwards	8 Sherwood
	9 Hurst		9 Gronow
	10 Brown		10 Fenwick
	11 Van Rooyen		11 Clark
	12 Roffey		12 Naylor
	13 Price		13 Stamper
Reserves	14 Walford		14 Schofield
	15 Coldrick		15 Schofield

Referee: H. HORSFALL (Batley).
Touch Judges: G. Dobson (Barrow) and G. Ireland (Widnes).
Schoolboys' Match, 1st Round Wood Cup: St. Marks (Red) v. National.
Wigan Schoolboys v. St. Helens Schoolboys.

The inside of the programme from February 23rd 1924, showing the teams of the day. Howley scored two tries, and Hurcombe, Ring and Price one each. Sullivan kicked six goals.

On February 14th 1925 Cumbrian amateurs Flimby and Fothergill arrived at Central Park in the first round of the Challenge Cup. They left without scoring, but Wigan managed 116 points, including a record seven tries for Johnny Ring and 22 goals for Sullivan. Sullivan's record remains intact, but Martin Offiah and Shaun Edwards have since managed 10 tries in a match.

The Wigan team that won the Challenge Cup for the first time back in 1924. In the Final at The Athletic Ground, Rochdale, Wigan beat Oldham 21-4. Back row (left to right): McCarty (trainer), Coldrick, Hodder, Roffey, Jerrom, Van Rooyen, Hurst, Brown, Fishwick (trainer). Front row: Van Heerden, Ring, Owens, Parker, Howley, Sullivan, Webster, Banks. Inserts: Price, Hurcombe.

The Wigan RL directors proudly show off the 1924 Challenge Cup, the first time Wigan won the tournament.

Full-back Jim Sullivan with the Challenge Cup in 1924.

The following season Wigan won the championship again, beating Warrington 22-10 at St Helens, with Ring scoring a hat-trick. That year Central Park was chosen to stage a Test match, the first of a series of games between Great Britain and New Zealand. The home side won 28-20 in front of a lowly 14,500 supporters.

Wigan 116 Flimby and Fothergill 0
February 14th 1925

THIS St Valentine's Day massacre produced a final score that set records – but Wigan fell three points short of the all-time biggest score – Huddersfield's 119-2 win over Swinton Park Rangers in 1914.

Flimby and Fothergill: Ritson, Peel, H. Atkinson, T. Ackerley, Robley, J. Ackerley, B. Atkinson, Richardson, Lewis, Holliday, Davidson, Irving, Little.

The Cumberland side arrived at Central Park for the first-round league Cup tie boasting an unbeaten record for the season with a defence that had let in just one try throughout the campaign. Wigan helped themselves to 24 tries.

Sullivan kicked 22 goals, Johnny Ring scored seven tries, and the rest of the touchdown list reads: Van Heerden 4, Booysen 3, Hurcombe 3, Price 3, Van Rooyan 2, Howley and Beetham.

When Wigan's score reached the century mark they ran out of digit space on the scoreboard and had to use Flimby's part of the board. Conveniently, the visitors failed to score.

Wigan: Sullivan, Ring, Howley, Hurcombe, Van Heerden, Owens, Booysen, W. Banks, Beetham, Burger, Roffey, Van Rooyen, Price.

Scrum-half Danny Hurcombe, who Jim Sullivan reckoned was one of the finest players he had ever played alongside. Hurcombe scored 56 tries in his 165 league appearances between 1919 and 1925, and was known for his pace, tackling and quick thinking.

Johnny Ring, who regularly got on the Wigan scoresheet between 1922 and 1932. He was the league's leading try-scorer for four consecutive seasons and only once did he score less than 30 in one campaign! He scored almost 400 tries for the club, and three times scored seven in a game.

Johnny Ring, seen here on the ball with Jim Sullivan looking on in the background, signed on August 23rd 1922 from Aberavon. The winger scored a total of 366 tries for Wigan between 1922 and 1932.

The New Zealand side that toured England in 1926-27, here pictured in front of the Dutch Barn. The Kiwis beat Wigan in their tour match 36-15 on December 11th 1926.

Wigan's Challenge Cup campaign ended at the first hurdle in 1928 when Huddersfield came to Central Park on February 11th and won 13-2. Here, Wigan's Lou Brown is tackled while Frank Stephens looks on. Behind them is the Kop end.

Central Park also hosted the 1927 and 1928 Challenge Cup, but of course the home side was playing no other part! In the first, Oldham were playing their fourth consecutive Final and beat Swinton 26-7 with 33,448 paying £3,168 4s 6d to watch. Swinton won in 1928, beating Warrington 5-3 in front of a similar-sized crowd. There was controversy at the time over the

The season ticket book for the 1927-28 season.

Wigan beat Halifax 14-5 in the second round of the Challenge Cup on February 22nd 1930. Wigan's Lou Brown tries to evade the tackle by Smith

A season ticket for Central Park dating back to 1927-28.

The Wigan Rugby Football Team, Wembley 1929. These were the first players to play the Challenge Cup Final at Wembley, when Wigan beat Dewsbury 13-2.

Another action shot from Wigan v Halifax, February 22nd 1930. Halifax's Gill is about to take the ball but Roy Kinnear is poised to tackle him.

choice of ground, but Central Park proved it was up to the job. Meanwhile, Wigan won the 1928 Lancashire Cup when they defeated Widnes at Warrington 5-4.

In 1929 there were more developments made to the ground, with terracing at the Pavilion end and banking at the Spion Kop, raising the capacity of the stadium. But Wigan were to go to a far grander stadium when they played Dewsbury in the Final of the Challenge Cup. For the first time the game was played at Wembley and, in front of 41,500 fans, Wigan beat Dewsbury 13-2 with tries from Syd Abram, Roy Kinnear and Lou Brown, and two Sullivan goals.

On March 8th 1930, the Central Park attendance record was shattered again when 39,003 people

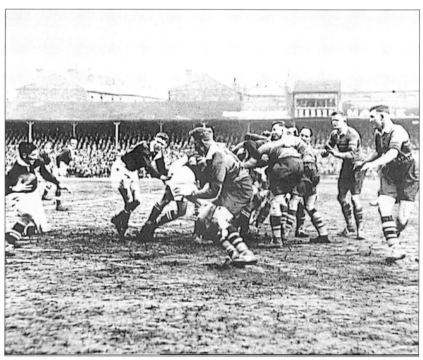

Wigan was used for Challenge Cup Finals twice before Wembley became the regular venue, in 1927 and 1928, and here, in 1932, because Wembley had been pre-booked for an England v Scotland football match. Leeds beat Swinton 11-8 in front of 29,000 fans. Here, Bryn Evans (Swinton) is well covered by the Leeds' forwards. Central Park later staged a Challenge Cup first leg game featuring Wigan and Bradford in 1944.

watched Wigan knock Warrington out of the Challenge Cup with a 16-5 win. The following year the stadium was used to stage a Championship Final for the first time, when Swinton beat Leeds, and the Challenge Cup Final the following year, when Leeds beat Swinton! That Final was to be at Wembley, but the Football Association objected to a rugby match being staged there a week before the FA Cup Final.

By 1932 an enclosed press box was built on the roof of the Douglas Stand, giving more room for spectators and a better vantage point for the press. The 'eagle's nest' was reached by a staircase from the path alongside the river. It was extended in the 1950s.

Central Park became the first rugby league ground to entertain royalty when the Prince of Wales, later Edward XIII, visited on November 23rd 1932. He watched a demonstration game featuring unemployed youngsters, but apparently was unimpressed with the ground. "It isn't a very good ground, is it?" he reportedly told Jim Sullivan – who presumably kept quiet.

A prince at Central Park. The picture shows HRH The Prince of Wales (later Edward VIII) visiting Central Park on November 23rd 1932, and chatting with Jim Sullivan.

Wigan and a France XIII team on Saturday March 10th 1934.

France played their first professional game of rugby league at Central Park, narrowly losing to Wigan by 30-27, on March 10th 1934. The union players, led by Jean Galia, had been persuaded to try rugby league and the Wigan match was the first of six games.

1934 saw Wigan lift the championship trophy once again. The team, skippered by Sullivan, beat Salford at Warrington 15-3. But Wigan were beaten finalists in the Lancashire Cup in 1934, 1935 and 1936.

Back at Central Park, concreting work began underneath the Dutch Barn and in front of the Douglas Stand, while the turnstiles on the Pavilion side were improved. The record crowd was broken again on March 21st 1936 when Central Park staged a Challenge Cup semifinal for the first time.

Joe Wilson, Jim Sullivan and Hector Gee, taking a break during a 1930s training session. Gee made 353 appearances for Wigan between 1932 and 1944, scoring 73 tries. Wilson, an Australian centre, made just 53 appearances between 1932 and 1934.

The Wigan RL team in 1935. That season Wigan reached their second Lancashire Cup Final in a row, but as in the previous season, ended runners-up. It was the same story the following year.

An aerial shot taken in 1938. The crush barriers are just railway sleepers and the original Dutch Barn and Douglas Stands are shown, as well as the old pavilion building, hen pen and scoreboard. The factory seen bottom left is Ranson's mill.

Wigan 23 Australians 25
November 3rd 1937

AUSTRALIA fielded a strong Test side for this game but their poor form in England meant that there was a poor crowd at Central Park – but how those fans who did not go must have regretted it!

Gwynne Davies repeated Jim Leytham's feat of scoring a hat-trick against a touring side but despite his efforts Wigan were to lose the match in a tense thriller.

The tourists took the lead through Pierce, scoring in the corner, but Wigan hit straight back when Davies took an inside pass from Holden to score.

Morley scored for the home side to put Wigan ahead and a Sullivan penalty made the score 10-3. A run from the halfway line to the goal-line under the sticks gave Norman a try for Australia and Williams converted.

In the second half Norval powered past Sullivan to give the visitors a

Jack Morley was a prolific try-scoring winger of the 1930s. He scored 223 tries in his 292 games for the club between 1932 and 1939.

one-point lead, but Davies scored for Wigan and Sullivan converted.

Aussie skipper Prigg, who was injured earlier in the game, scored the third Australian try but Davies scored his third straight after and Sullivan converted. At this stage the score was 20-14 and Wigan looked set for a win.

Heidke scored for Australia but when Morley retaliated for the home side and there were only six minutes remaining, Wigan were still very much the favourites to win.

Yet with one minute to go Prigg scored again and Norval produced an outstanding try straight from the re-start. The scores were level and Australia's Beaton had a difficult conversion kick – but he put the ball over the crossbar for a memorable win.

Wigan: Sullivan, Holder, Bennett, G. Davies, Morley, Garvey, Gee, Edwards, Golby, Banks, Thomas, A. Davis, Jones.

Australians: Ward, Dawson, Beaton, B. Williams, McKinnon, Norman, P. Williams, Stehr, Pierce, Heidke, Norval, Lewis, Prigg.

Centre Gwynne Davies made 300 appearances for Wigan in the 1930s and scored 127 tries. He scored a hat-trick against the Australians in 1937.

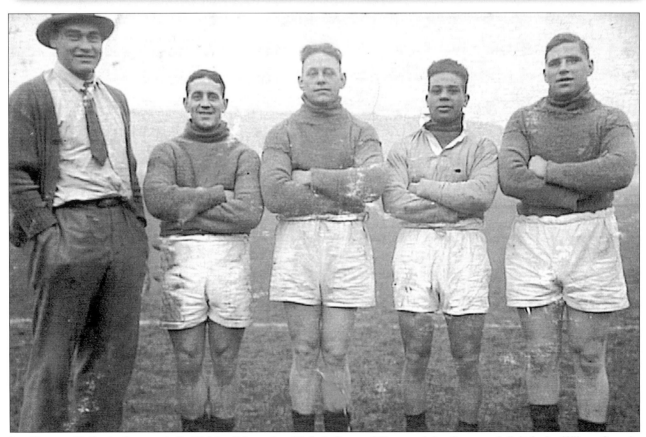

Len Mason with Hector Gee – or is that Va'aiga Tuigamala with Andy Gregory? The remaining three are definitely Joe Wilson, Georgie Bennett and Harold Edwards – all players from the 1930s.

In October 1938 Harry Sunderland, the Australian touring team manager, took over as secretary-manager at Wigan RL. Here he imparts his knowledge to the players.

Jim Sullivan with the 1938 Lancashire Cup. It was his five goals that won the final against Salford at Station Road on October 22nd.

Sullivan is seen here in 1939 with secretary-manager Harry Sunderland.

Skipper Jim Sullivan is shown here in the Central Park dressing room, talking tactics to the Wigan players in November 1939.

Warrington beat Salford 7-2 in front of 41,538 spectators.

During the 1937-38 season a touring group of Cossacks staged a horse riding display, while in August 1938 the first annual charity game between Wigan and Warrington was held. The score was 17-17 but Warrington took the trophy by winning the toss of a coin. Later that year Wigan won the Lancashire Cup, beating

Joe Egan

Joe Egan was brought up in the St Patricks parish district of Wigan, played his amateur rugby for that club and had a brief spell at Wigan Highfield as a teenager in their open age side. They never signed him, but fortunately Wigan saw his potential and they did. This was in 1937.

The following year Egan was used at hooker – a problem position for Wigan – and he was in and out of the first team until World War Two. He was renowned for being a great player in the loose, and as skipper in the post-war years he was greatly responsible for one of Wigan's most successful eras.

In all, he made 362 appearances for the club.

Egan helped Wigan end their 19-year Challenge Cup drought in 1948 and enjoyed the distinction of being the first player to receive the trophy from a reigning monarch, King George VI. That is one of his most treasured memories, but in all his reminisces it is only natural that he should keep on returning to his 'second home', Central Park.

"Fortunately I only played five games for Highfield and then I signed for Wigan," Egan recalled. "It was very difficult. I didn't know much about the organisation, about how these things were supposed to work. There was nobody about to advise you on what to do. But you didn't bother about the money anyway – it was the honour of playing for the club that you lived and breathed."

Egan signed for £20. After he had played three first team games he earned a further £25 and for an international call-up an extra £25 went into the account. But at first it was not all plain-sailing.

"Sometimes I wouldn't even get into the second team. Some weeks I would play in the reserves and other weeks I would not get a game at all. It was really frustrating. I would work all week and even on Saturday mornings and all the time I couldn't wait to play."

A brass moulder by profession, Egan would learn on the Monday evening what the following week's team would be. By Tuesday the teamsheets would be passed round the pubs, and many people would talk of nothing else all week. "They experimented at hooker with a player called Albert Davis. But I got my first game against Leigh at the old Mather Lane ground (October 8th 1938), and I think I was lucky really in that the player opposite me didn't have much experience either. I did well enough that day.

"The following week we played Halifax at Central Park and I was pitted against an international Welshman. I came second against him but I was able to cover that up with some loose play, that rubbed the shine off his performance a bit.

"The following week was the Lancashire Cup Final against Salford, who were one of the mighty teams of that time, and they had previously beaten Wigan three times in the Cup Final. I was selected for this one, but it was no credit to me that we won the match (10-7 at Station Road). Jim Sullivan kicked five goals. The strange thing about it was I was dropped after that! But it was of no consequence to me because I had played in a Lancashire Cup Final for Wigan and I was only 19 years old – it was an exceptional achievement at that time."

Egan finally made the hooker position his own during the truncated season of 1939-1940 as the war broke out. Wigan had no fewer than 13 experienced Welshmen in their side and many returned to their country to sign-up for the Army. It gave the local boys a chance to shine.

The war's effect was not lost on Egan. "The war made a difference," he admitted. "The pre-war team was packed with experienced players and it was difficult to get in. The club re-built during the war and it produced a great side, a successful side that played great rugby league."

As well as playing rugby at Central Park, Egan marched

Joe Egan in full flow during the 1950 Australia tour. Egan made 362 appearances for Wigan between 1938 and 1949, later captained the side and then coached the team between 1956 and 1961.

Coach Joe Egan returned to Central Park in 1956 and here he discusses Cup tactics. Personnel include Keith Holden, Bill Bretherton, John Barton, Brian McTigue, Billy Boston, Frank Collier, Dave Bolton, Fred Griffiths, Frank Wright, Mick Sullivan and Eric Ashton.

with the Home Guard soldiers along the Popular Side terraces. The ground was used as a base for the local Home Guard during the war years, and there was even a small anti-aircraft gun mounted at the Kop end.

"I used to report to Central Park for the Home Guard, and march up and down the terraces. If we were not allowed on the pitch we used to march along the Popular Side terraces. They had a gun on the Spion Kop – this was when there was no shelter there. They just dug a hole into the embankment big enough for the gun and a couple of soldiers. It was supposed to be an anti-aircraft gun but it wasn't very big – I don't know what value it had. I remember that a bomb dropped only 50 yards from the ground, on Greenough Street."

Games during the war years tended to be eventful. Egan remembers catching the train to get to Knowsley Road and then walking from the station – and getting lost. "The game kicked off 20 minutes late but nobody minded." He also remembers ex-Wigan Highfield player George Davies being sent

off in a Boxing Day derby match against St Helens and referee Bill Stockley being rushed to safety by the Wigan players after an angry pitch invasion. The game was abandoned after 57 minutes, but Wigan were credited with a 12-3 win.

Egan, as player and coach, worked alongside many other great players. For Jim Sullivan he had the highest praise. "I can only say good about him. Sully was a great mixer, a keen golfer. He had a good sense of humour. He was a great player we could all look up to.

"During the war he didn't always want to play, he was getting older and lacking the enthusiasm. But he used to come back in the big games, the Cup games or the play-offs, and kick goals for us! He could kick from anywhere in the field. One of his great assets as a coach was that he could see how the game was developing and how it was different from his day. Instead of trying to make us do it in his style he let us develop and pushed it further in that direction.

"Ken Gee was the perfect man for his position.

He was a hard man, a strong man – a pit man. He had a great sense of humour, and he was a brilliant goal-kicker as well.

"But they were all good players, a local team that was started during the war. The team was so strong and that was fully reflected by 1950 when we had eight players selected for the tour of Australia."

After a spell at Leigh, Egan returned to his beloved Wigan as manager-coach in August 1956. In his second season he guided Wigan to the Lancashire Cup Final but they lost to a very strong Oldham side. In the following two years he brought Challenge Cup success to Wigan and in 1959-1960 the club won the Championship. When Wigan lost to St Helens in the 1961 Challenge Cup Final, it was Egan's last match in charge of the cherry and whites.

"On reflection, coaching must be one of the worst jobs there is," Egan said. "There were always about 15,000 or 20,000 people who knew more about it than you did. But I enjoyed it. It was very difficult, but it wasn't as bad then as it is now. Nowadays you can toss a coin and get sacked on the result.

"When I came back in 1956 the team was struggling a bit but we got things together again. Coaching Boston and Ashton was easy, really. They were such talented players, generally speaking it was just a case of fitting the team together and keeping the whole thing harmonious."

Egan believes that Central Park's location will be one of the main reasons why the ground will be missed. "It was a communal place," he said. "When I used to go there as a fan we used to walk, and we knew all the walls to jump over. Central Park was home from home, and my first memories are of the ground. I am going to miss it terribly."

Salford 10-7 at Station Road in the Final.

In 1940, after the outbreak of World War Two, the ground became a training centre for the Home Guard, the Territorial Army and the Training Corps. Anti-aircraft guns were positioned on the Spion Kop while the pitch was used for drills, the space beneath the Douglas Stand became a soldiers' billet and one of the dressing rooms was used as a temporary jail!

In 1941 Wigan entered the Yorkshire Cup for the first time, with the Lancashire Cup suspended. Leeds came to Central Park and won 9-3.

A number of rugby union clubs played at Central Park during the war – Lancashire played Yorkshire in charity matches for the British Red Cross Society, and rugby league players were allowed to take part. In April 1943 the Royal Air Force played the Combined Services in aid of the RAF Benevolent Fund.

Baseball came to Central Park on October 10th 1943 when United States Army officers formed two teams for a demonstration match. The California Eagles took on the New York Yanks, and the Yanks won 19 runs to seven.

By the 1940s a game was played at half-time involving youngsters in the crowd. While the players drank from bottles of water by the touchline, hundreds of lads would pour onto the field and start a game of 'keep-ball'. The boy in possession would run round the field while everyone else went after him, and he would hold onto the ball for as long as he could without being caught before booting it into the air and letting someone else take the lead.

In 1944 Wigan reached the two-legged Final of the Challenge Cup. They beat Bradford Northern 3-0 at Central Park in front of 22,000 supporters but lost 8-0 away. The war ended a year later and six years of neglect at the ground meant

more money had to be spent on the ground. But Wigan's fortunes on the pitch meant that money would not be a problem.

Post War Boom

Wigan won the championship in 1946, 1947, 1950 and 1952, and their success combined with a post-war optimism brought huge crowds to Central Park. The team

Tom Bradshaw, scrum half for Wigan between 1939 and 1951. A great playmaker, he made over 300 appearances and scored 35 tries.

Two great players of the 1940s and 1950s, Tom Bradshaw and Ces Mountford.

Ken Gee, wearing his distinctive headguard, approaches the action. He joined the club in October 1933 and played his final game almost 21 years later, and in that time he played a key role in the successful pre and post-war sides. Gee was a big but quick prop, with great handling. It took him two years to break through into the first team and he went on to appear in 10 Lancashire Cup Finals, winning it seven times. He was also a Great Britain international and won two Challenge Cup and two Championship medals after the war. He and Joe Egan were a great double act. In all, he scored 54 tries and kicked 508 goals in his 559 appearances.

Stand-off Ces Mountford captained Wigan to victory in the Championship in 1950 and in the Challenge Cup in 1951.

was studded with stars – Ernie Ashcroft, Martin Ryan, Tom Bradshaw, Ken Gee, Joe Egan, Brian Nordgren, Jack and Billy Blan and Ces Mountford. In 1946 they beat Huddersfield at Maine Road 13-4 in front of a huge 67,136 crowd, and the following year 40,599 watched Wigan defeat Dewsbury 13-4 at the same stadium. Huddersfield lost 20-2 to a depleted Wigan side at Maine Road in 1950 – 65,065 saw that game in what many believe was Wigan's greatest triumph – and two years later 48,684 saw Wigan lift the trophy again, this time disposing of Bradford Northern 13-6 at Huddersfield.

Martin Ryan, an attacking full-back who signed in 1940. He made 300 appearances, scored 67 tries and kicked 63 goals. He played his last game for Wigan at Workington in 1952, but later served on the board of directors.

The Challenge Cup Final team in 1946, a Final Wigan lost to Wakefield by just one point.

Ken Gee. An amateur rugby knockout tournament for Wigan clubs was named after him, and its final matches were held at Central Park.

Brian Nordgren, 'Noggie' as he was known, seen here in training at Central Park. The Kiwi sprinter came to Wigan in 1945 and scored 312 tries in his career for the club. Also a useful goalkicker, Nordgren could have formed a lethal wing pairing with Billy Boston but in 1954 he returned to New Zealand to become a solicitor.

Joe Egan leads the team out against Barrow on December 28th 1946. This picture shows the old pavilion building, before it was extended, and also the board which a youngster would carry round the touchline to show the fans what changes there were to the side. The four changes for Wigan in this game were Nordgren, Cunliffe, Ashcroft and Atkinson.

A famous picture from 1946, when Wigan played Bradford at Central Park. The ground already looks packed yet there are hundreds more

...g to get through the turnstiles.

Groundsmen clear snow and slush from the Central Park ground during March 1947. The Kop end is in the background.

Two years after Wigan lost to Wakefield at Wembley in the Challenge Cup, they went back to the capital and beat Bradford 8-3. In 1951 they beat Barrow 10-0 in front of 94,262 spectators to lift the trophy again.

In 1946 more work was done at Central Park, including more concreting, and a new wall with turnstiles and exit gates was built across the front of the ground. The following year a public address system was installed, featuring six speakers fixed to the pavilion at the back of what was known as the hen-pen. It was used for the first time on March 12th when Wigan played Carcassonne. Wigan

Kiwi Wiganer Ces Mountford greets the Kiwi tourists on October 22nd 1947. In a tight match, the New Zealanders edged the game 10-8.

The team that beat Widnes 11-3 at Central Park on March 15th 1947. Ernie Ashcroft scored two tries and Brian Nordgren one.

The Wigan side that beat Halifax 30-5 on May 17th 1947, including a hat-trick for Ces Mountford. The team is Atkinson, Nordgren, W. Blan, Cunliffe, Shovelton, Barton, Banks, Ashcroft, Tracey, Ward (captain), Mountford, Lawrenson and J. Blan.

The Wigan team that played New Zealand Tourists at Central Park on October 22nd 1947. The team is: Bowen, W. Blan, Ratcliffe, Barton, Ward, Nordgren, Ashcroft, Ryan, Egan (capt), Bradshaw, Gee, Mountford, Banks.

lost 11-8, but more significantly French full-back Puig Aubert 'took a leak' on the centre spot just before kick-off!

A new scoreboard, in memory of Bert Jerkins, was erected during the 1947-48 season at a cost of £2,000, featuring team names and scores on rollers that was believed to be the first of its kind in rugby league. The scoreboard also provided a clock and displayed half-time scores for other games.

In that same season Wigan attracted an average attendance of

Wigan bring the Lancashire Cup back to Central Park on November 1st 1947 after beating Belle Vue Rangers at Wilderspool 10-7. Nordgren and Ratcliffe were the try-scoring heroes.

The February edition of the Rugby League Review 1949 features Central Park on the front page. The picture shows the Leytham-Jenkins Memorial Scoreboard and Pavilion.

27,000, and at the end of the year Wigan County Borough Council's Parks Department was employed to work the pitch.

A fire broke out in the directors' box in the championship play-off semi-final against Bradford Northern on April 28th 1948. Thought to be started by a cigarette, it was quickly put out by the fire brigade and fortunately the structure was not badly damaged. Wigan went on to lose the game 15-3.

The Wigan team that beat Warrington 6-3, with a single try for Ernie Ashcroft, on November 22nd 1947. The line-up for that day was Ryan, Nordgren, Roughley, Ashcroft, Ratcliffe, Mountford, Bradshaw, Gee, Egan, Barton, W. Blan, White, Hudson.

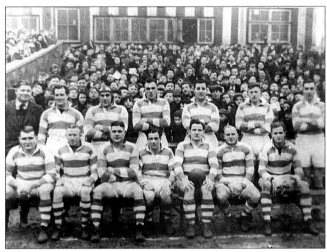

The Wigan team that beat Widnes 8-5 on January 24th 1948. Back row (left to right): Sullivan (coach), Ryan, Gee, W. Blan, Ward, Hilton, Bowen. Front: Banks, Lawrenson, Barton, Bradshaw, Egan, Mountford, Ratcliffe.

The Wigan team before they played Leeds on March 6th 1948. Back row (left to right): Barton, Ashcroft, Ward, White, Ratcliffe, Hudson, Hilton. Front: Ryan, Gee, W. Blan, Egan (captain), Bradshaw, Mountford. Wigan won 41-6.

Pemberton Secondary Modern School Rugby Team 1948-49 season. Back row, from left: Brian Bradshaw, Eric Fisher, Gerry Ainscough, Tom Foster, Jimmy Birkett, John Smith. Sitting: Bill Jones, Ken Croston, Arthur Gregory (captain), Harold Gregory, Tommy Baird. Kneeling: Eric Topping, Billy Kilshaw. Arthur Gregory is the father of Andy Gregory and Harold is Andy's uncle. This team lost to All Saints, which featured Norman Cherrington, in the Final of the Wood Cup at Central Park by 3-2. Cherrington scored the only try.

Johnny Lawrenson, seen here scoring one of his five tries against Halifax on March 20th 1948 – a game Wigan won 55-0 – made 219 appearances for Wigan and scored 187 tries and 128 goals in that time. His career was interrupted by the war when he served with the RAF. He moved to Workington for the 1949-50 season but later returned to Central Park in a coaching capacity.

Wigan against St Helens, March 26th 1948. The picture shows Saints defending their line, with the Dutch Barn in the background.

The same game, and once again Wigan are on the attack. Ernie Ashcroft, on the ground, looks on, and Tom Bradshaw is seen furthest away. Wigan won the game 22-11 thanks to a hat-trick from Fred Barton, a try from Billy Blan and five goals from Ted Ward.

The Australians entertain the Central Park masses with their pre-match war-cry, October 20th 1948. Wigan beat the tourists 16-11.

Ken Gee proudly stands by Wigan's trophy haul in the 1940s. The picture also shows how the crush barriers used to be made out of railway sleepers.

The Wigan team that defeated Belle View Rangers at Central Park 48-5 on December 4th 1948. Back row (left to right): Ryan, Barton, White, Gee, Ratcliffe, Hudson, Ward, Blan. Front: Ashcroft, Alty, Lawrenson, Egan (captain), Mountford.

The first all-ticket game at Central Park was held on April 9th 1949 when Wigan beat Warrington 26-7, in front of a capacity crowd of 42,500. It was Wigan's third successive win over the Wire and the belief was that Warrington were terrified of playing Wigan. "If they just threw 13 cherry and white jerseys on the ground and let Warrington kick off," one fan told the *Wigan Observer*, "I'll bet a pound to a penny they would knock-on before they reached the line."

Concreting work continued on the terraces and iron crush barriers replaced the wooden ones and remained in place until 1987 when they were deemed unsatisfactory. In February 1949 land at the rear of the Spion Kop was used for the

A then record crowd at Central Park of 42,500 for the all-ticket clash between Wigan and Warrington on April 9th 1949. Wigan won 26 7.

The coaching team at Central Park in April 1949.

first time as a training ground, to reduce wear and tear on the pitch. Also that year the wooden fence that went round the pitch was replaced with a concrete wall, with dug-outs to house reserves, training staff, first aid people and police.

Bench seats were part of the wall and allowed 500 fans to get close to the action, used for the first time when England met Wales in March 1950. Opposing teams' benches were originally either side of the field, until the dug-out below the

Douglas Stand was divided in two for both teams.

On April 7th 1950 the Good Friday derby match against St Helens, which Wigan won 17-12, attracted a record attendance of 44,529. Ten days later eight of

A movie still that shows the turnstiles and the old forecourt at the pavillion end.

A movie still showing fans queuing for tickets for Wigan's third round Challenge Cup game against Barrow in 1949. Places were limited at Barrow – but those who left this queue disappointed did not miss much – Wigan lost 8-7!

The queue for the Challenge Cup game at Barrow in 1949.

Wigan's coaching team at Central Park's gymnasium, inside the old pavilion building, in April 1949.

Action on the try line during Wigan's 45-14 Lancashire Cup first round win over Oldham on August 27th 1949.

Another star-studded Wigan team from after World War Two. Back row (left to right): Ted Ward, Ken Gee, Brian Nordgren, Frank Barton, Les White, Bill Hudson. Front: Martin Ryan, Billy Blan, Joe Egan, Johnny Lawrenson, Jack Cunliffe, Tommy Bradshaw, Cec Mountford.

The first Whitehaven team to go to Central Park in a first-team fixture, October 1st 1949. Wigan won 43-2 with hat-tricks for Brian Nordgren and Ernie Ashcroft.

Wigan's players went on tour to Australia, but Wigan kept on winning and lifted the championship trophy on May 13th at Maine Road, a measure of the depth to their squad. On August 26th 1950 an Italian side made its rugby league debut at Central Park, losing 49-28 to Wigan at the start of a six-match tour. That month Wigan became the first rugby league club to have uniformed commissionaires on matchday duty.

In 1951, the forecourt outside the pavilion was resurfaced and plans were drawn up for a new stand that would replace the

Wigan 13 Leeds 12 September 7th 1949

A GAME made memorable by an epic run by stand-off Ces Mountford, who stole the match from Leeds with a try in the final seconds of the game.

Mountford suffered an injury during the game and had retired to the bench, but with Wigan trailing 12-10 with less than a minute to go, something had to be done. Coach Jim Sullivan threw him into the fray.

Wigan had a scrum just inside their own half. Mountford took the ball from Tom Bradshaw and the Kiwi star began a superb swerving run over to the left.

He ignored Brian Nordgren, who was waiting for a pass on the left, but used him as the perfect foil.

Ces Mountford scores a terrific try for Wigan to pinch a win against Leeds on September 7th 1949.

Brian Nordgren scores one of Wigan's three tries in their 13-12 win over Leeds on September 7th 1949.

With the Leeds defence expecting a pass to 'Noggie', Mountford went straight through to score. Thanks to that great effort, one that fans talked about long after, Wigan won the game 13-12.

It was Mountford's second try of the game. Nordgren also touched down, and Gee kicked two goals.

The Wigan team that day was: Ryan, Ratcliffe, Broome, Ashcroft, Nordgren, Mountford, Bradshaw, Gee, Egan, Barton, Silcock, Slevin, Hudson.

Another capacity crowd at Central Park for a Good Friday derby clash, April 7th 1950. Wigan beat St Helens 17-12 thanks to tries from Billy Blan, Ces Mountford and Brian Nordgren. Ken Gee kicked four goals.

Worsley Boys Club became the first youth team to play in the first round of the Challenge Cup. The game was staged at Central Park and despite a brave display, they lost to Hunslet 45-7.

Left: Winger Brian Nordgren beats the last man on his way to the try line.

Below: Brian Nordgren goes in to score one of his two tries against York in the first round, second leg Challenge Cup game on February 11th 1950. Wigan won the first leg 38-2 at York and at Central Park they beat the visitors 65-15.

A club record number of players selected for a rugby league tour of Australia in 1950. The seven were Martin Ryan, Jack Hilton, Ken Gee, Tommy Bradshaw, Joe Egan, Jack Cunliffe and Ernie Ashcroft, pictured here with a suitably happy coach Jim Sullivan. An eighth was added as a late replacement – Gordon Ratcliffe.

Another view of the crowd in that 1950 derby game.

The Mayor of Wigan meets the Wigan side at Central Park before they defeated a touring Italian side 49-28 on August 26th 1950.

Two days after the Italians had been vanquished, the Mayor greets the Wigan side before their 72-29 victory over a Welsh touring team.

Gordon Ratcliffe scores a try to the delight of his fellow players in a capacity crowd thriller. According to Jim Sullivan, Ratcliffe was his favourite winger. He played for Wigan between 1944 and 1953, scoring 185 tries in his 212 appearances.

Wigan 48 Huddersfield 13 on September 9th 1950, here showing Nat Silcock poised to make the tackle. He scored two tries in the game, as did Nordgren, Mountford and Roughley.

Wigan's haul of trophies in 1950 – the Lancashire Cup, Ward Charity cup, League Cup and the Challenge Cup.

Tom Bradshaw, sitting on the ringside seats in front of the hen-pen. His son Rodney is sitting next to him.

Dutch Barn, but post-war building restrictions meant that an application had to be made to the Ministry of Works.

Between 1951 and 1977 the Central Park pitch was featured in seed catalogues, such was the quality of the surface. This was down to head groundsman Bill Mitchell, who was appointed on September 1st 1951. Even the groundsmen at Wembley stadium sought his advice!

On January 12th 1952 the TV cameras were at Central Park for the first time, as Wigan took on Wakefield Trinity. The BBC, which only showed the first half of the match, had two cameras posi-

Central Park before the Spion Kop was covered in 1954 – the aerial photograph also shows part of the housing estate where Central Park Way now runs. The mill has gone and Calderbank's scrapyard – at the bottom of the picture – fills the space.

The Wigan team for the 1951-52 season.

The Wigan team v St Helens on Good Friday 1951. Wigan won 22-13 with two tries each from Mountford and Slevin, and one apiece for Ashcroft and Nordgren.

Jack Hilton is shown here, determined to beat the Warrington defence and score – unfortunately he fell short. Ken Gee and Ted Slevin are the Wigan players in the background. Wigan won this postponed league match on April 16th 1951 by 19-2.

Billy Mitchell was Wigan's best known groundsman. He was appointed as head groundsman on September 1st 1951 and retired 25 years later, by which time he was known throughout the country. He was an expert at growing grass, the Central Park pitch featured in seed catalogues, and even the groundsmen at Wembley came to him for advice! Chairman Ken Broome presented him with a carriage clock to mark his 25th year at the club in 1976. He retired not long after but continued to lend his experience to his successor.

Coach Jim Sullivan and Tom Bradshaw walking out at Central Park.

The cover of the matchday programme, March 1st 1952. It was a Challenge Cup second round game against Bradford Northern and Wigan won 28-12. Brian Nordgren scored a hat-trick.

Dai Bevan heads for the line with Jack Fleming and Ernie Ashcroft in support. This picture was taken in the early 1950s.

Wigan Welsh winger Dai Bevan, scoring one of his 45 tries in just 59 appearances between 1951 and 1953.

Jackie Cunliffe is tackled by the Workington defence, watched closely by Wakefield referee Ron Gelder. Cunliffe was a great all-rounder – he signed for Wigan in December 1939 and played his last game for the club in January 1960. He made 447 appearances in all, scoring 85 tries and kicking 371 goals.

Wigan v Bradford Northern in1952. Jack Hilton leads the team out at Central Park.

Brian Nordgren goes in for his hat-trick try against Hull in the 1952 Championship semi-final. Wigan won the game 13-9 and beat Bradford Northern 13-6 in the final to clinch the championship.

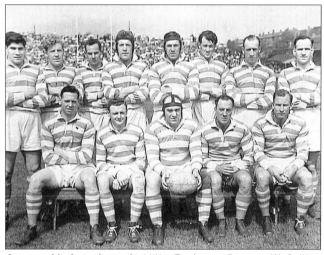

A great side from the early 1950s. Back row: Broome, W. Collier, Bevan, F. Collier, Street, Williams, Mather and Cunliffe. Front row: Ashcroft, Kelly, Gee, Fleming and Nordgren.

Bill Sayer goes after Vince Karalius with Brian McTigue looking on, in another great Wigan – St Helens derby.

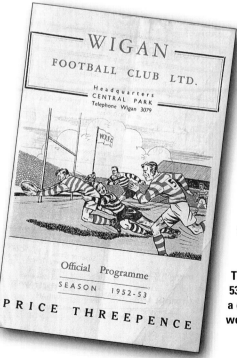

The matchday programme in the 1952-53 season. The cover was dominated by a cartoon drawing while advertisements were confined to the inside.

tioned on the Douglas Stand. Wigan won 29-13 and, despite the TV coverage, 17,974 went to see it.

On April 11th 1952 St Helens came to Central Park and 44,674 fans watched Wigan squeeze a win by 15-11. That summer the pitch was improved for drainage and the training pitch behind the Kop was enlarged. By September a licence had been granted from the Ministry of Works for a new stand on the Popular Side, and the club was considering installing floodlights. A canteen was built at the rear of the Dutch Barn but this was destroyed in a fire a few years later.

By 1952 the great side began to break up and Wigan began a period of rebuilding. Yet it was this era that would produce the next batch of Wigan 'legends.'

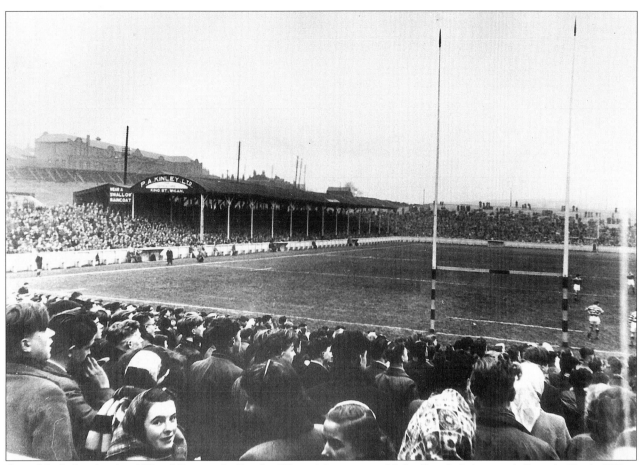

Central Park showing the old Dutch Barn on the Popular Side and the uncovered Spion Kop. A shelter was built on the Kop in 1954.

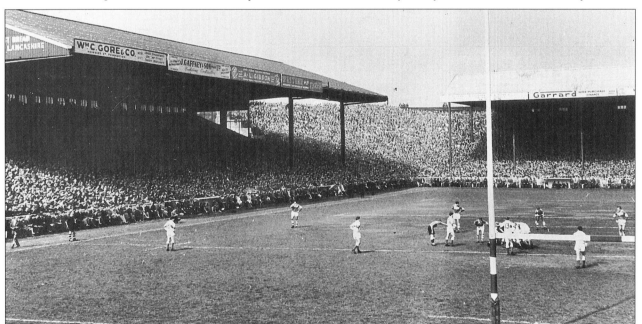

Central Park in 1960, showing the New Popular Stand. The Dutch Barn was demolished in 1954 and a new stand erected by August that year.

The Boston Era

Billy Boston signed from Cardiff RU in May 1953. He would go on to become the club's all-time greatest try scorer and one of the great legends of the game. His time at the club coincided with a period of interest in the sport that was never equalled, before or since. But towards the end of his Wigan career, in the later 1960s, fortunes for the club began to dwindle once again.

Symbolic of the club's success was the construction of the Popular Stand. In 1954 the Dutch Barn was demolished and a new

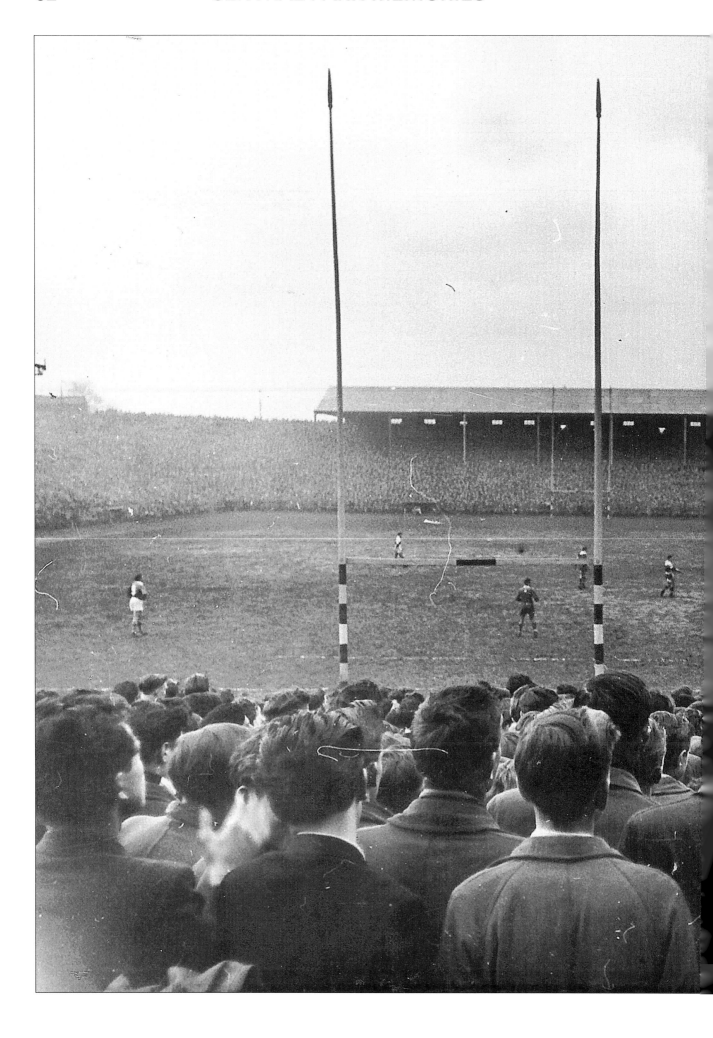

stand built in its place so quickly that it was ready by the start of the next season. It was opened on August 21st when Hunslet came to Central Park and were beaten 16-6 before 14,275 fans. The stand was imaginatively called New Stand, until 1972 when the New Douglas Stand was built, when it became known as the Popular Stand. The game against Hunslet was also the first to have commentary broadcast to local hospitals. Harry Sunderland, the BBC sports commentator at the time, presented the game.

Billy Boston OBE

WILLIAM John Boston signed from Tiger Bay for £3,000 on Friday March 13th 1953, although his dad didn't

Billy Boston emerges from the tunnel at the Pavilion End for the first time and begins a glittering career at Central Park. Here he is making his debut for the A-team, against Barrow A, on October 31st 1953. More than 8,000 people went to see it.

Billy Boston scores his first try for Wigan's first team, against Barrow, on November 21st 1953. Wigan won the match 27-15.

want him to go. Boston had scored 126 tries in just 30 games playing Union for the Royal Signals Catterick team and rugby league clubs took note. Wigan beat Workington and Hunslet in the race to sign him, and his capture was kept secret until his Army service had ended. Wigan put up fly-posters advertising his first game, for Wigan A against Barrow A at Central Park on October 31st 1953.

Boston recalls, "One of the best moments I had at Central Park was one of the first. I played for the A-team against Barrow A, and the first time I

Billy Boston equalled Wigan's record number of tries scored in one match – previously held by Johnny Ring and Gordon Ratcliffe – with this touchdown against Dewsbury on August 20th 1955. He also scored seven against Salford in April 1962.

touched the ball I scored a try. I didn't have to beat anybody to the line, but it was great all the same!

"I made my debut about a fortnight after for the first team, also against Barrow, and I played on the left wing. I remember scoring a try in that match, and after about six games I got picked to go on tour to Australia. It was a bit of a shock because at that stage I still didn't know how to play the ball! I learned how to do that in one of the team hotel's corridors in Sydney.

Billy Boston in good form against Oldham at Central Park on September 1st 1956, a first round Lancashire Cup game. Oldham sneaked it 18-16.

"But it all happened so quickly and it was a fantastic start to my rugby league career."

Boston scored 478 tries from 487 Wigan appearances, 571 tries from 564 rugby league games in all and between 1954 and 1963 he garnered 31 Great Britain caps in total, scored 24 tries in those games, and also had Welsh representative honours.

Boston added, "I continued to score tries, and when I put a bit of weight on I learned how to use a shorter side-step and did some more body-work. I always scored a few every season – around about the 50 mark – so it wasn't bad!

"I remember playing Leeds in a Cup tie, though I don't recall what year it was. It was late on in the game when me and Eric Ashton did this move and scored under the sticks. Our players, not normally ones to get ecstatic, were jumping up and down.

"I think most of my best memories are from Central Park. I never played any good games at Wembley – things just didn't run right. They were not bad, but I thought they were nothing more than average – especially when you are looking forward to having a good game.

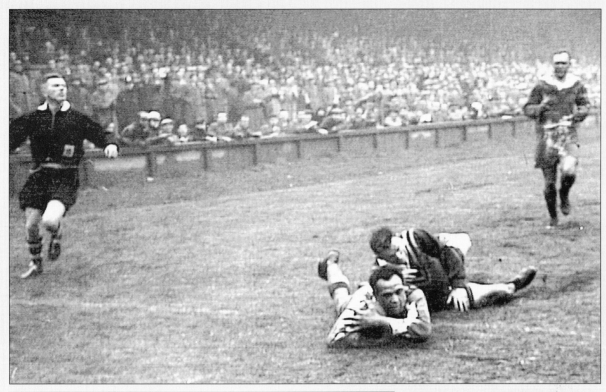

Boston scores a try despite a desperate late tackle by Australia's 'Bandy' Adams. Eric Ashton was the other man to score as Wigan's famous double act helped to beat the Australians 16-9 at Central Park on November 14th 1959.

"I think the best game I ever had was at Leeds in the Challenge Cup (February 9th 1957). I scored two length-of-field tries but we lost 13-11. I remember Eric Ashton had this kick to level the scores – he kicked it and it was going straight between the sticks, but the wind took it outside.

"I also remember playing against St Helens at Central Park when they had the record crowd – 47,000. The fans were literally standing shoulder to shoulder and the noise was incredible.

"I remember we played Leeds in a Cup tie and we drew five-apiece (February 11th 1961). We played

Billy Boston emerges from the tunnel for Eric Ashton's testimonial match at Central Park on Whit Monday, May 26th 1969.

Billy Boston was unstoppable at full pelt, here outstripping the covering defence to score another great try.

Billy Boston – one of the greatest players the game has ever seen.

the replay at Central Park on the Wednesday and there were headlines in the local papers that if anyone had any time off work they would get sacked. It was a sell-out, so there must have been a few sackings the day after!

"That was Eric's favourite game as well – because he got sent off! It was my fault. Me and the second row forward Fairbanks for Leeds had been having a tussle. I'd played at centre the week before but in the replay at Central Park I was put back on the wing,

Boston scoring against Rochdale Hornets – Dave Bolton's in support but he's not needed.

Boston scores a try. This photograph also shows the straw at the side of the pitch which was used to cover the pitch pre-match so that it wouldn't freeze.

Billy Boston – In his rugby league prime.

so I waited and waited and when I got the chance I crash tackled him.

"He was bit dazed but then Eric came over and said, "Get back on the wing, Billy." I went back and when Fairbanks looked up he saw Eric, had a pop at him and they both started fighting. Off they went. I don't think he's ever forgiven me for that."

Apart from topping the league's try-scoring list in 1956-57 with 60 touchdowns, Boston had to wait until 1958 for his first club honours – a Challenge Cup winners' medal. He won a Championship medal the year after – his two tries helping to beat Wakefield Trinity in the Final – and in 1965 he won a second Challenge Cup medal when Wigan beat Hunslet. His final medal came courtesy of Wigan's 16-13 win over Oldham in the Lancashire Cup in the 1966-67 season. The following season he retired after an arm injury.

Boston will be most remembered by his adoring fans for his try-scoring genius at Central Park, and he admits the ground will be missed.

"Central Park is like a shrine to me, and always will be. Like a second home. They might have rebuilt it but even then it probably would not have been the same. We have to move with the times."

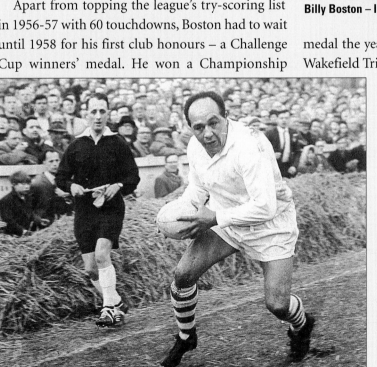

Boston in a familiar position – about to score another try.

In 1996 Billy Boston was awarded the OBE – he had just returned from Buckingham Palace when this photograph was taken.

Also in 1954 a shelter was built on the Spion Kop and used for the first time when Wigan lost 9-5 to Oldham on November 27th. Four years later the shelter was extended and, other than the crash barriers being upgraded, the Kop remained unchanged.

A record attendance of 44,731 was set on April 12th 1956 in a replayed Challenge Cup game

David Bolton was one of the best half backs to don both Wigan and Great Britain jerseys. He made his first game at the age of 17 and went on to make 300 appearances, scoring 127 tries between 1954 and 1963.

Brian Nordgren emerges from the Central Park tunnel for the last time. His last home game was against Barrow on March 12th 1955. He kicked a goal but Wigan lost 12-11. Behind him in this picture is Tommy Parr.

between St Helens and Oldham. A year later the club launched the Wigan Rugby Development Fund, a weekly lottery with cash prizes that aimed to raise money for Central Park. The draw has been run, under various names, ever since.

At the end of the 1956-57 season the public address system was destroyed in a fire, so a large speaker was fixed to a pylon at the score-

Brian McTigue made 422 appearances for Wigan between 1950 and 1966, scoring 44 tries. He started his Wigan career at centre but took his great handling skills to prop forward. He could have gone into boxing, and Wigan were on the brink of selling him to Oldham after he spent three years playing in the reserves. All who saw him play are glad neither of those things happened. He had 21 Great Britain caps.

Brian McTigue stands eighth in the club's all-time appearance list with 422 games.

board end. Plans to extend the damaged pavilion were approved and the boardroom with its large window overlooking the hen-pen was built. This later became part of the players' bar, and later still it became the vice-presidents' lounge.

The great Ernie Ashcroft ended his career in 1958 but by this time Wigan had found another excel-

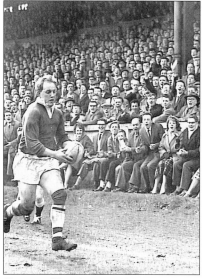

Norman Cherrington, Wigan's international second rower, who scored a sensational try at St Helens on March 9th 1957. He's about to get another one here, to the delight of the Central Park crowd. Cherrington made 257 appearances for Wigan between 1953 and 1961, scoring 80 tries.

Brian McTigue looks on as Norman Cherrington grounds the ball over the try line.

Terry Entwistle, Brian McTigue and Bill Collier in a spot of light-hearted training.

lent side. Brian McTigue was well into his 400-plus match career for the cherry and whites, and he would be joined by Mick Sullivan, Dave Bolton and Frank Collier – who, along with McTigue, helped to make the Wigan pack one of the

Roy Evans signed for £200 from Spring View in 1957 and made 282 appearances for the cherry and whites until 1965. He played in four challenge cup finals, toured Australia in 1962, and won four Great Britain caps. He scored 34 tries for Wigan.

Ernie Ashcroft is shown here with Eric Ashton in the Central Park dressing room. Ashcroft signed for Wigan 10 years before Ashton but the two graced the field together between 1955 and 1958.

Fred 'Punchy' Griffiths, a full back who made crunching tackles. His brilliant goal technique brought 663 goals from just 161 games. He scored an amazing 394 points in the 1958-59 season alone. His Wigan career spanned five years between 1957 and 1962.

October 1957 saw the arrival of Mick Sullivan, greeted here by Billy Boston and Eric Ashton. Sully enjoys his first sausage, bacon and eggs, Wigan's first customary after training.

Geoff Lyon joined Wigan from Orrell RU at the age of 18. He was a running forward and a good finisher, scoring 73 tries in his 302 games between 1959 and 1969.

most formidable in rugby league at that time. Together with the double act of Boston and Eric Ashton, Wigan were entering another successful period in their history.

Work on the stadium reflected this. In 1958 the roof over the Spion Kop was extended and, completed the following year, meant 20,000 spectators were now under cover. At the start of 1959 a bar was opened under the Popular Side stand – originally 70 feet long, the bar became known as the Sullivan Bar.

It was 1959 that could have proved the final straw – for the straw. Up until that year straw had been used to protect the ground from frost, but experts advised Wigan that laying straw caused long term damage to the turf. After the club stopped using it, the short term effect was that games had to be postponed because of the weather. So the straw was brought back!

On March 27th 1959 Wigan beat St Helens 19-14, despite the visitors fighting back from 14-0 down. But the game is better remembered for the attendance – 47,747. It is almost now certain there will never be such a huge crowd for rugby league – or any sport for that matter – in Wigan again.

Long before undersoil heating, straw was the answer to keeping the frost at bay. Before every match there was the ritual of collecting the straw and stacking it beyond the touchlines.

Wigan 19 St Helens 14
March 27th 1959

The great derby game of March 27th 1959, when 47,747 crammed into Central Park. Eric Ashton, the Wigan skipper, is caught by Duggie Greenall and Dave Brown while Alex Murphy, Jan Prinsloo and Brian McTigue look on.

Griffiths kicked twice to give the home side a 4-0 lead and Evans scored the only try of the first half, which Griffiths converted to make the score 9-0.

Eric Ashton combined with Billy Boston for the Welshman to score, and when Griffiths goaled it looked as though Wigan were on course for a straightforward victory.

But Saints hit back through Alex Murphy and Smith, and the score became 14-8. Ashton picked

MADE famous because of the attendance, Central Park's all-time record of 47,747. A total of £4,804 went into the club's coffers that day.

Wigan and St Helens were at the top of their game, and this eagerly awaited match lived up to expectations.

Referee Eric Clay signals play on as Alex Murphy spins the pass out to the St Helens full-back.

Keith Holden makes a break for Wigan with Dave Bolton in support on the inside.

up a loose ball to halt the decline and Griffiths converted, but the game was not over yet.

A controversial refereeing decision allowed Greenall to touch down and Prinsloo added a further score for Saints to bring them right back into it.

Sullivan and Boston linked up and almost produced a try in the dying moments, but Van Vollenhoven halted the move with a great tackle. Wigan hung on for the win.

Wigan: Griffiths, Boston, Ashton, Holden, Sullivan, Bolton, Thomas, Bretherton, Sayer, Platt, Cherrington, McTigue, Evans.

St Helens: Moses, Van Vollenhoven, Greenall, Howard, Prinsloo, Murphy, Smith, Brown, Bowden, Briggs, Terry, Huddart, Karalius.

Later that season Wigan went to Wembley and won the Challenge Cup for the second successive year. In 1958 it had been a 13-9 win over Workington Town – this time Hull were vanquished 30-13. They would also be beaten finalists in 1961 and 1963. But in 1960 Wigan won the championship

South African scrum-half Tommy Gentles scores a great try in Wigan's 38-0 win over Rochdale Hornets on April 4th 1959.

Central Park in 1960 showing the ringside seats around the pitch. The seats, which went round three sides of the ground, were first used when England met Wales in March 1950.

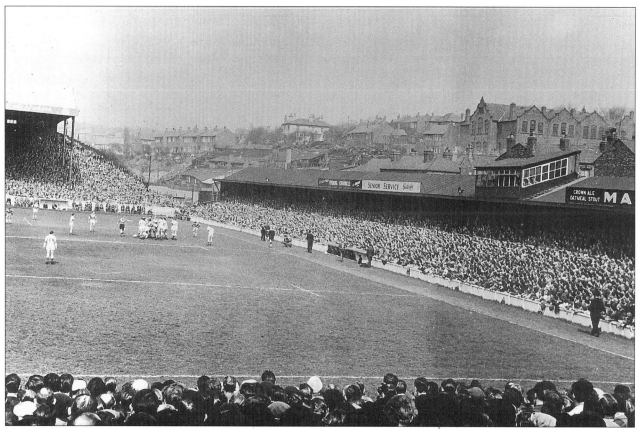

Another big crowd at Central Park, shown here in 1960. The Douglas Stand, with its rooftop press box, was knocked down in 1973 and rebuilt.

Wigan against Leigh at Central Park in 1960. Brian McTigue and his colleagues are about to join the scrum.

Wigan stalwart Brian McTigue, here playing against Leigh in 1960.

Billy Boston straps up before the game. This picture was taken in 1961.

The Good Friday derby clash on March 31st 1961. Wigan beat St Helens 12-2. The picture shows Terry Entwistle well tackled by Large. Boston, Carlton and Bootle are in view. Eric Ashton and Norman Cherrington were Wigan's try-scorers that day.

for the ninth time, beating Wakefield at Odsal 27-3 in front of 83,000 fans!

At the annual general meeting in 1959 chairman Bill Gore announced that a new Douglas Stand costing £100,000 would be built when sufficient funds had been raised. By 1961 nothing had happened but the club re-stated its desire for the new stand, but a year later a 'continental' style stand costing £110,000 was proposed, and expected to be completed within

Wigan's hopes for the 1961 Challenge Cup Final. Back row (left to right): Barton, Evans, McTigue, Boston, Sayer, Lyon. Front row: Collier, Griffiths, Entwistle, Bootle, Ashton (captain), Carlton, Bolton.

Central Park, February, 1962. Wigan coach Griff Jenkins talks tactics to Frank Carlton, Frank Parr (obscured), Dave Bolton, Fred Griffiths and Eric Ashton.

three years. The cantilever construction would extend over the River Douglas, would seat 5,000 and raise the ground capacity to 55,000. New terracing at the front would be built and £20,000 spent on dressing rooms beneath the stand.

Meanwhile, padding around the goal posts was used for the first time in the Test match between Great Britain and Australia at Central Park in December 1959, following an injury at another ground. This soon became stan-

dard. In 1960 Central Park became a World Cup venue for the first time when Australia beat France by 13-12, and New Zealand beat France 9-0.

In 1961 the dressing rooms, baths and showers were modernised and new entrances were built at the Whelley corner.

In September 1962 the Wigan Rugby New Stand Fund was launched to raise money for the Douglas stand project, but a row erupted at the 1963 annual general meeting when directors admitted some of the money raised had been spent on new players. Also, the path along the River Douglas was a 'right of way' and Wigan's plans to build an extended stand on that side were halted at the planning stage.

By the 1964-65 season tipping

The Wigan line-up in 1963 looked like this. Back row (left to right): Barton, Lyon, Boston, McTigue, Gregory, Collier. Front: Carlton, Evans, McLeod, Ashton (captain), Pitchford, Bolton and Davies.

had begun behind the Kop and the Colinfield car park was used for the first time on August 26th when Wigan played Blackpool Borough.

Groundsmen working on the ice during the big freeze in 1963.

In 1963 the ice breakers were busy with their pneumatic drills trying to break up the Central Park 'ice rink' at Wigan when the club's Fijian signing Kia Bose arrived on the scene – for his first slide on ice. Wigan were out of action for 10 weeks because of the big freeze.

Then in 1965 work began on the social club – it was opened on May 23rd 1966 and cost £20,000. It was later known as the Riverside Club.

Since 1965, BBC2's Floodlit Trophy had been growing in popularity but by 1967 Central Park was still in the dark. The four 120ft pylons that stood at the ground until its final days were constructed, each fitted with 36 1.5kw lights, and those and the lights for stands, turnstiles, toilets and exits were wired up to a new sub-station for Central Park. Regarded as the best

Trevor Lake makes the tackle at Central Park. Lake made 140 appearances for Wigan between 1962 and 1966, scoring 132 tries.

floodlights in the game, the total cost came to £17,500.

The big switch-on was a nightmare. Wigan invited unbeaten league leaders Bradford Northern

Colin Clarke strikes a pose for the camera, and looks remarkably like his son Phil. Clarke played for Wigan between 1962 to 1977, scoring 75 tries in his 431 appearances. He joined Wigan as a 17-year-old from Orrell RU, and showed great skill as a hooker. He was famously suspended for the 1965-66 Challenge Cup final, but had won a Wembley medal the year before at the age of 19. He played for Great Britain and returned to Wigan in a coaching capacity in 1984 for two years.

Brian McTigue and Eric Ashton (left) keep an eye on the action in this Central Park battle against Featherstone Rovers.

Colin Clarke is poised to cut off the Featherstone Rovers' pass.

New Zealand on the attack in a Test match against Great Britain at Central Park.

to Central Park on September 26th 1967 and the game was heralded by the Scots Guard Association Pipe Band, and kicked-off by pop star and Wigan fan Georgie Fame. Lord Derby, president of the Rugby League, switched on the lights but in the second half more than 12,000 fans and two rugby teams were plunged into darkness.

Foreman Colin Stanton of Elequip electricians revealed £17,500 worth of state-of-the-art illumination failed because of leaky rubber washers! The fans made the most of the blackout by lighting matches and cigarette lighters in the darkness while the Scots Guards did a hasty rendition of *Hieland Laddie*. After emergency repairs had been carried out, the lights at the Pavilion end worked and the match was played to a 7-all draw.

After that the floodlights worked fine and Wigan entered the Floodlit Trophy, winning it in 1968-69 beating St Helens 7-4 in the Final – the first of three Finals to be held at Central Park. In 1968 Billy Boston ended his competitive career with Wigan following a serious injury to his arm. Then Eric Ashton ended his playing days in 1969 and continued to coach the team until 1973, when he went to Leeds for a short spell before moving on to St Helens.

Cliff Hill gets back to his position, here in action against Hunslet. Hill made 179 appearances for Wigan between 1964 and 1970, scoring 57 tries.

Official programme for the Wigan versus Warrington game in 1966. Photographs had replaced cartoon drawings on the front cover.

The Lean Years

The 1970s would get off to a good start. Wigan reached the Challenge Cup Final in 1970 but lost to Castleford, and in 1971 they finished runners-up to St Helens in the Championship but won the

Eric Ashton MBE

Eric Ashton scoots in for another try – 1960.

Eric Ashton began his career with Wigan in 1955 and on November 11th 1963, after a trial period, he was appointed coach. During his playing days the centre scored 231 tries for Wigan,

kicked 448 goals and amassed a total of 1,589 points in his 487 appearances.

Like Jim Sullivan before him, as a coach he was a disciplinarian but also knew that words of encouragement for his players worked just as well as a loud ticking-off!

He joined Wigan after just playing 40 minutes of a public practice match at Central Park in August 1955, after learning his rugby with St Helens' B team.

Following a few appearances for Wigan he was selected to play for Lancashire and received a surprise call-up for the Great Britain World Cup team in 1957, a tournament in which he starred. The following year he was made vice-captain of the British side touring Australia.

As a player he led Wigan to six

Eric Ashton in practice at Central Park.

Eric Ashton scoring against Hull at Central Park on September 14th 1968. Wigan won 22-9.

Wembley appearances and once again took them to the twin towers as coach. In his later years at Central Park the team was blighted with injuries and trophies slipped by them. In 1971 his club created a record by remaining undefeated for 31 consecutive league matches.

In 1966 he was awarded an MBE for his services to the game – the first rugby league player to receive honours. It was befitting of the great man.

His first game for Wigan was at Central Park on August 20th 1955, scoring two tries in Wigan's 52-5 win over Dewsbury in front of a 10,000 crowd. It was a debut that would be overshadowed by Boston's seven-try haul, but given that Ashton had been thrown straight in at the deep end, it was a start that promised much.

He said: "Officially my first competitive game was a Ward charity game against Warrington (August 13th 1955) and I had to defend against Brian Bevan, a real Willow the Wisp. I thought I did

Ashton after scoring his last try for Wigan on May 3rd 1969. Wigan lost the play-off match against Salford by 26-21.

Eric Ashton leaves the Central Park pitch after Wigan lost the second round of the Championship play-offs against Salford at Central Park on May 3rd 1969. It was his last competitive match, and fans applauded him off the field.

Eric Ashton MBE was presented with this shield by the directors of Wigan RL after his retirement in July 1969.

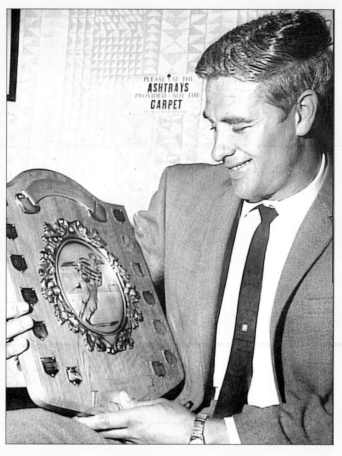

alright – I wasn't overawed because I had nothing to lose.

"I scored two tries in the Dewsbury game, so I got off to a decent start. I played on the left wing then, and on the other wing Billy scored seven tries. I had already heard of Billy, of course, and it was a thrill to be playing on the same side as him."

His selection for the first team after only one trial

The players formed a guard of honour and the crowds applauded as Eric Ashton left the Central Park pitch for the last time on May 26th 1969.

Eric Ashton and Billy Boston, with referee Mr Davies from Manchester, just before the kick-off for Ashton's testimonial. In the match programme, chairman Ken Broome wrote: 'Eric Ashton will always be remembered by RL followers the world over for his part in the incomparable partnership with Bill Boston. But Wiganers know him as a truly great player in his own right.'

game had divided the Wigan directors, some of whom favoured a Cunliffe-Broome left wing partnership. But as the Wigan Observer noted, "Ashton more than justified his selection… and also showed useful goal-kicking powers."

Ashton believes the big crowds helped the team to be more focused and more successful, and in particular helped himself and Boston. There was rarely less than 15,000 at Central Park, and more often there were more than 20,000 in the ground. Games against Warrington and St Helens attracted more than 40,000.

"I think what helped myself and Billy more than anything was playing in front of such tremendous crowds. There would be nothing too unusual about 30,000 or 40,000 people at Central Park, and that created a brilliant atmosphere.

"Even if they get a good crowd of 12,000 or 15,000 now, back then the crowds were often treble that. The atmosphere was marvellous – crowds like that made the players.

"Central Park was marvellous, there were not many grounds like it. I liked to play at Leeds and St Helens as well, but when you played at Central Park it was the tradition that struck you. It had seen so many great players – Joe Egan, Ken Gee, Jim Sullivan, Johnny Ring, Hector Gee – you were fighting to keep up with the great players that had gone before you.

"My favourite game has to be the 1959 Good Friday derby against St Helens when there were 47,000 fans at Central Park. Incredible. It was a sweltering day and possibly I have the most vivid memories of it. Running out onto the field was unbelievable and you couldn't hear yourself think. Then people in the town would talk about the game all week."

He recalled the time he was sent off after clashing with George Fairbanks of Leeds in a midweek afternoon match, in front of 43,000 fans. Billy Boston had clouted Fairbanks but when the Leeds man got up and played the ball, he thought it was Ashton who'd dished out the rough treatment and gave some back. Both he and Ashton walked. "I spoke to

Billy afterwards," Ashton recalled, "but it's not for repeating here!"

His combination with Boston is as legendary as both players in their own right, but it was only in the latter half of the 1955-56 season that Ashton played centre to Billy's wing position. Only injuries forced them into different positions after that, of course.

"It was just something that came with experience," Ashton said. "We just got used to playing together, we knew when to come inside, when to kick the ball. We played together for years and it only came after a period of time. When people look back at things they tend to think that we just hit it off straight away, but I think it took time."

Ashton's first experience as a coach was in helping Johnny Lawrenson in 1961, when Lawrenson was caretaker coach, replacing Jim Sullivan who had been struck down with illness. Ashton's reign at the helm was as successful as Sullivan's post-war effort, bringing the club a Challenge Cup triumph in 1965 and the League Leader's Trophy, the Lancashire League, two Lancashire Cups and the 1968-69 Floodlit Trophy.

Despite the success, Ashton said it paled when compared to playing. "There's no substitute for playing," he said. "When I was coach we won quite a few things, so I cannot grumble. Being a coach takes so much involvement on all levels, as well as taking stick from the media! But coaching is second-best compared to playing. It's easy to talk a good game but you want to be out there playing it."

Ashton is one of the few people who has a big involvement in the two great rival camps. For that he has made many friends in both towns, but, as he admitted somewhat jokingly, there have always been some who have seen him as a traitor.

"I've never been able to win," he said. "As a St Helens lad when I played for Wigan they hated me in St Helens. Then when I went to St Helens and later got on the board they hated me in Wigan!"

Lancashire Cup Final that year and again in 1973. They would then have to wait until 1977 for another Final appearance – a Lancashire Cup game in which they finished runners-up. They did this again in 1980, but that was quickly over-shadowed by the infamous 1979-80 season, when the club was relegated to Division Two. Wigan rugby league was at its lowest ebb.

Central Park in the late 1970s. The main additions to the ground are the social club at the Pavilion end and the floodlights. The shelter over the Kop end had been extended in 1958.

Geoff 'Piggy' Fletcher at Central Park. Bill Ashurst and friends used to have fun with his wig in the dressing room.

The Wigan team from 1970 lined up as: Robinson, Tyrer, Wright, Clarke, Burdell, Ashcroft, Ashurst, Mills, K. O'Loughlin, D. Hill, Laughton, Parr, Rowe, C. Hill.

Off the field, work finally began on the new Douglas Stand, but plans for a double-decker cantilever building were scrapped

Wigan skipper and coach Eric Ashton signs autographs for a group of schoolboys from Marseilles, who played a series of rugby league games in the Wigan area in 1969.

A shot of the crowd at the Douglas Stand end for Eric Ashton's testimonial game – two youngsters get star billing!

Doug Laughton, here showing a great set of teeth, played between 1957 and 1962, scoring 38 tries in his 183 appearances. Laughton won most of his honours with Widnes in the mid 1970s.

Colin Tyrer boots for goal. A fine full-back, he amassed 1,890 points in his 8-year Wigan career. He played between 1966 and 1974, scoring 88 tries and kicking 813 goals in his 246 appearances.

because of falling attendances, and poor performances on the field meant that many believed the money would be better spent on new players.

The building of the new Douglas Stand was a long and, ultimately, tragic affair. Planning permission was granted in November 1971 but the club was not allowed

This is an artist's impression of the new £100,000 Douglas Stand at Central Park. It gives some idea of how smart Wigan's ground will look in future years. Designed by architects Michael Connell and Bernard Popland, A.R.I.B.A., of Manchester, the stand should be the last word in spectator comfort.

CHANGING FACE OF CENTRAL PARK

An artist's impression from 1972 of the new £100,000 Douglas Stand.

The old Douglas Stand and the 'eagle's nest' press box.

to close the footpath along the River Douglas as this was a right of way. E. Ayles and Son were awarded the £92,000 building contract as the best deal of six tenders, a company run by Wigan director Eric Ayles. Costs rose as a large amount of concrete had to be laid in the foundations – a problem that later haunted the building of the Whitbread Stand.

The old Douglas Stand was

Inside the old Douglas Stand press box. It was built into the roof of the Douglas Stand in 1931 and accessed by a staircase at the rear. The Eagle's Nest, as it was known, was extended in the 1950s.

The old Douglas Stand when it was demolished after the 1971-72 season. The wooden construction had stood since before the First World War, with extensions and seating added to it.

demolished at the end of the 1971-72 season. At the same time, the terraced houses on the far side of the river were being knocked down and the scene was one of total dereliction. Central Park almost looked unrecognisable. On May 26th 1972 a driver shortage meant that Eric Ayles himself decided to lend a hand on the Douglas Stand site. Tragically, as he drove a tipper lorry through the gateway at Central Park it dislodged a concrete lintel weighing three tons. It fell onto the cab and crushed it, killing Mr Ayles. A popular man, he had served on the board for three years.

On May 26th 1972 tragedy struck. Wigan director Eric Ayles, whose construction company was building the new stand, was killed when a slab of concrete crushed the cab of the truck he was driving. Mr Ayles had been helping out because there was a driver shortage. He was 44.

A month later his firm collapsed and Allen Brothers were brought in to take over the work. The new season started with the stand still not complete, and by now the cost of the project had risen to more than £100,000. Hundreds of fans watched games from the footpath on the far side of the River Douglas, getting a great view without having to pay!

The new stand was opened on January 14th 1973, providing 1,500 seats, a press box, and a director's box which had wider seats than the others in the stand. It was called the New Douglas Stand, but this clashed with the Popular Side's

Construction on the new Douglas Stand. It cost more than £100,000 to complete and was several weeks behind schedule. While it was being built fans could watch the games from the other side of the River Douglas free of charge!

Doug Laughton leads the team off Central Park after Wigan's 15-2 defeat over St Helens in the second round of the Challenge Cup on February 18th 1973. Laughton was one of Wigan's try-scorers that day.

New Stand, so that was renamed the Popular Stand!

In the 1970s the concrete wall which went round the pitch, providing ringside seats on three sides, made way for advertising hoard-

The new Douglas Stand nears completion, and secretary Geoff Douglas tries out one of the seats. It was finally opened to the public on January 14th 1973.

RUGBY LEAGUE
CHALLENGE
CUP
2nd ROUND

AT CENTRAL PARK, WIGAN
WIGAN
versus
ST. HELENS
Sunday, February 18th, 1973
Kick-off 3-0 p.m.

'B2 SECTION'
60p
SECRETARY

Admit One
New Douglas
Stand
ROW C
Waterside Entrance

RESERVED
SEAT
No 18
STARRS LTD

Tickets like these were hot property when the New Douglas Stand opened in 1973.

ings. It was found that adverts made more money than premium-priced seating for those who wanted to be close to the action.

As Wigan's fortunes on the field continued to plummet, improvement work on the stadium went on hold and a bare minimum was spent on the ground's maintenance and upkeep.

In 1974, though, Central Park was back in favour for staging big, neutral games. The Clubs' Championship Final – a play-off competition featuring the best-performing 16 clubs of the season – took place at Central Park between St Helens and Warrington. The Premiership was introduced the season after, and the first Final of that competition was staged at Central Park when

George Fairbairn models some stylish knitwear in 1974, seen here with Wigan chairman Norman Bibby.

Full-back George Fairbairn in action against St Helens, tracked by Harry Pinner (right) and Billy Benyon. Fairbairn made 204 appearances for Wigan between 1974 and 1980, kicking 583 goals and scoring 30 touchdowns.

A frozen pitch, despite the use of covers. The photograph also shows the eagle's nest television gantry in the Douglas Stand before it was extended at the request of John Monie, so he could have unhindered views of the action.

Leeds beat St Helens 26-11. The finals later moved to Old Trafford and the Premiership was played up until the Grand Finals were introduced in 1998.

Bill Mitchell, Central Park's well-known groundsman, celebrated 25 years at the club in 1976 and was presented with a carriage clock by chairman Ken Broome – he retired shortly after but continued to help his successor. In November that year the groundsman's store-

room in the Popular Stand was converted into a gymnasium, work costing £3,000. Also during 1976 the club made plans to hold a market every Thursday on the Colinfield car park, but Wigan Metro quickly ruled it offside, referring to an ancient charter that

Former St Helens player and coach Joe Coan joined Wigan in January 1975, pictured here for his first game in charge with, left to right, Tony Karalius, John Gray, Brian Gregory, Brian Hogan and Colin Clarke. Coan left Central Park the following year.

gave them the sole right to stage markets in the town. The market was only held once.

In January 1977, after 13 years' service at the club, assistant groundsman Tommy Jackson retired. The *Observer* noted: 'Tommy's slightly-built figure is a familiar sight at Central Park on match days, doing a dozen and one jobs with Billy (Mitchell), and then collecting tickets outside the tea-room at the end of the day.' A special leaving presentation was made for him.

Also that month the social club was re-named the Riverside club and John Martin, who had compered at Fagin's nightclub in Manchester, became the manager and host. The cabaret club was brought to life and it remained popular right up to the last act.

In 1980 the scoreboard operator's room was converted into a boardroom and bar, and the old, large boardroom was now used as a hospitality lounge and a vice-presidents' club. A temporary scoreboard was used in the window of the pavilion until 1985 when a new electronic display was installed.

More dressing rooms were built beneath the Douglas Stand in 1981 and a £12,000 extension was built onto the pavilion dressing rooms, completed early the following year. The pavilion's old tea-room became a players' lounge and the Wigan Hall of Fame.

But developments at Central Park were overshadowed by what was happening on the field. Wigan were relegated at the end of the 1979-80 season, and although they bounced straight back into the top flight, it was clear that rebuilding was more urgently needed on the pitch rather than off it.

Bill Ashurst

Bill Ashurst signed as a 19-year-old centre from Wigan Rose Bridge in 1968 and some people thought he would become the next Eric Ashton. He eventually played in the second row and was one of the most imaginative players of his time. His strong running, tackling, handling and goal-kicking skills were first class, and his 74 tries and 146 goals from 179 Wigan appearances reflected that.

Ashurst was part of the side that won 31 consecutive league games, from February 28th 1970 to February 5th 1971, and won the Harry Sunderland trophy in the Championship Play-off Final defeat against St Helens at Station Road. He played in the 1970 Challenge Cup Final defeat against Castleford, but received winners' medals when Wigan beat Saints in the Floodlit Trophy and when they won the Lancashire Cup, beating Widnes. He also won three Great Britain caps.

He had two spells as a Wigan player, moving to Penrith in Australia for a time, before signing for Wakefield in a then record £18,000 transfer deal.

Unsurprisingly, the record run of 31 league wins remains large in his thoughts but the lack of a trophy at the end of it still rankles, since Wigan lost in the Final of the Play-offs. He said: "We finished top of the league yet that was never recognised, and I still feel sorry for all the players about that. It all started

after we were beaten 53-11 by St Helens at Central Park (Boxing Day, 1969). We sat down after, decided we had to get into it and rolled our sleeves up. But I felt sorry for the likes of Doug Laughton, Colin Clarke, Bill Francis, Brian Hogan and Eddie Cunningham. People forget what we did that season."

He reckons his best individual performance came in the Centenary Game at Central Park, on November 17th 1972, when Wigan drew 18-all against a strong Australian side. The *Wigan Observer*

Local lad Bill Ashurst was a second row forward and a skilled goal kicker. In all he made 179 appearances between and 1968 and 1977, scored 74 tries and 146 goals. He never toured but got three Great Britain caps.

Bill Ashurst in action.

noted at the time that Wigan had produced their best form for years.

"I think Australia were unbeaten and we should have won it, too – we gave away two interception tries. I dropped two goals and created three tries, and I was recommended to Penrith after that. That was my best performance as a professional.

"But I also played at Central Park in a Ken Gee Cup Final for Wigan Rose Bridge. We played the Stork Hotel and there were 9,000 people there for the game. I remember we got a penalty straight from the kick-off, on the halfway line, and I went for goal. People were saying, "What does he think he's going to do?" but the ball went straight through, higher than the posts.

"I suppose the biggest highlight was when I was signed, back in 1968. Eric Ashton was my hero at the time and I never dreamed I would end up playing alongside him. My first game at Central Park was against Hull – a midweek game – and I scored a try in the corner. That was a great moment."

Ashurst also recalls funny moments from the dressing room, at the expense of two of his colleagues. Apparently, the signings of Geoff Fletcher and John Whittle were the cause of some fun in the back rooms.

"They both wore wigs," Ashurst explained. "We used to tie them to pieces of string and pull them around, or tie them to the pegs on the walls. It was really funny. Fletcher and Whittle got used to it – they had to!"

Bill Ashurst believes the Wigan supporters deserve a brand new stadium, and knows that although Central Park has gone, it will never be forgotten.

"Central Park has been a mecca for many rugby league fans. I think the supporters made it what it was – they were superb – and they will now have a superb new stadium. But perhaps the saddest thing is that children like my son, who play rugby league and love the game, will never get the chance to play at Central Park."

The Glory Years

No one knew as the 1980s progressed how one club was going to dominate so many competitions. The revolution started in the boardroom when an ungainly 10-man board of directors was reduced to four – Jack Hilton, Maurice Lindsay, Tom Rathbone and Jack Robinson. For them, money appeared to be no object, but they spent wisely and Wigan would reap the rewards for the next 15 years.

Wigan reigned in the Challenge Cup from 1988 to 1995 – an unprecedented feat in rugby league – and were similarly unstoppable in the championship. The team was stuffed with star players, many of whom became household names across the country. But while the fortunes of the team went through the roof, their home ground remained comparatively unchanged.

The latter half of the 1983-84 season was played with lop-sided goal-posts! On the day before Leeds were due to meet Widnes in the Final of the John Player Special Trophy gale force winds snapped one of the posts at the Pavilion end. Makeshift repairs meant one of the posts tilted until the end of the season. New posts were put in during the summer.

The season also ended with Wigan going to Wembley for the first time since 1970, but they lost in the Final against Widnes 19-6. Alex Murphy, who had begun to revive the fortunes of the club, was sacked before the start of the following season after a bust-up with Maurice Lindsay.

Alex Murphy

Alex Murphy has seen Central Park from all angles, from an opposing player or coach, to a Wigan coach and as a media representative. In the 1950s and 1960s Murphy's St Helens were involved in some titanic battles against the old enemy – few fans will forget the infamous double sending-off at Knowsley Road during the top four Play-offs in 1960, when both Murphy and Mick Sullivan received their marching orders.

But what was it like to play

Wigan were only just starting to come out of the doldrums when Warrington came to Central Park on September 20th 1981. They lost this match 22-11, and finished the season sixth from bottom – and were lucky to be that high up the table.

Alex Murphy, supported by Cenydd Williams, gets away from the Wigan defence in the derby game on April 16th 1965. St Helens won 16-8.

Wigan sparked into life under the coaching of Alex Murphy between June 1982 and August 1984. Here he receives a hero's welcome at the 1984 Wembley homecoming, despite Wigan losing to Widnes in the Final. Murphy was sacked before the start of the following season.

Alex Murphy shares a drink with his mud-splattered heroes after winning the John Player Special Trophy in 1983.

for the enemy at Central Park? Murphy remembers it well.

"Intense. Incredibly intense, but always great games. The important thing was what it was like to play against Wigan – it was the be-all and end-all, the derby game of all derby games.

"I remember when John Monie came here the first time and the board said to him: "We don't mind what you do, how many games you win, you must win on Boxing Day and Good Friday against St Helens." He'd only just stepped off the plane!

"The atmospheres at Central Park were tremendous – I remember going there and the gates were locked at 11am. There would be 40-odd thousand in the ground.

"The atmosphere was electric and there was always a lot of passion in the game. It was always won by someone who had a bit of class, or from a mistake – it was always that keen, and there was never a lot between the two sides.

"We would have a good run, then Wigan would have a good run – but the important thing was to win, no matter how.

"The supporters from both sides were absolutely magnificent – the Wigan supporters followed the Wigan lads, but they also appreciated the class on the other side as well.

"It wasn't just one-eyed support then – of course the fans wanted their own side to win – but they appreciated the class from all the players. They would also go to other clubs to watch great players – that doesn't happen anymore."

Murphy coached Warrington in the 1970s and was manager of Leigh before he coached Wigan between 1982 and 1984. Many people regard his short spell at the club as helping to provide the catalyst for the amazing years that would follow.

He said: "When I first came to Wigan as a coach the club was having a very bad time and I think what we achieved with what we had to operate with was not far from a miracle.

"We didn't have world-class players, we didn't have bags of cash to be throwing about, we had just come out of the Second Division and when I got to the club they were at a very low ebb. I signed Shaun Edwards on BBC television, and I think that was the start of things – up until then we had been losing all the kids. So I think we did very well with what we had, and we laid the foundations for what was to come."

Alex Murphy emerges from the Central Park tunnel, here as coach of Warrington.

Ironically, though, one of Murphy's fondest moments at the ground was a joke from the fans at his expense.

"I remember one time when I said something in the press about Wigan and pies. I can't remember whether I was at St Helens or Warrington at the time, but I remember when I got to Central Park all the supporters had made pies. One supporter presented me with the biggest pie you have ever seen in your life – it was like a birthday cake with a face on it.

"Central Park held some lovely memories for me, and it has always been a pleasure to go there. Everybody has got to move, but I think a lot of people will miss it."

Wash day at Central Park. Hanging out the dirty shirts are Alex Murphy and Dave Bolton. Hope they remembered to take it down before kick-off!

Alex Murphy in his media pundit days. "Was it something I said?"

Shaun Wane makes a break with Joe Lydon looking on. A local lad, prop forward Wane served the club for a decade from 1981 to 1991.

Graeme West in action. West signed for Wigan in 1982 and his strong running brought him many tries. He took up the coaching reigns after John Dorahy left in May 1994 but left in controversial circumstances in February 1997. He has since returned to the club in a scouting role.

In 1985 more improvements were made to the ground – a play-group and crèche was opened, and the floodlights were replaced. The bulbs were removed and replaced with 20 high-powered lamps on each of the existing pylons, costing the club £36,000. The new lights were used for the first time when the Roses match was staged at Central Park on September 11th.

The following month the electronic scoreboard was installed and a month later the club announced that under-soil heating would be provided at the stadium. Thanks to help from Norweb, the installation cost just £88,000.

Meanwhile, Colin Clarke and Alan McInnes jointly took over the coaching duties in August 1984

Shaun Edwards

A youthful Shaun Edwards.

Shaun Edwards has a run on the Central Park turf for the first time, in October 1983. His signing, on his 17th birthday, was filmed at midnight by the BBC's *Breakfast Time* cameras.

When Shaun Edwards signed for Wigan in October 1983 on his 17th birthday, it was a ceremony filmed for TV. The fee was reportedly a massive £35,000. Edwards was hot property even then, having skippered an English school side in league and union, but could he live up to this early stardom?

The short answer was yes, and the slightly longer version would later read: Three World Club Championship winners' medals, nine Challenge Cup triumphs, eight championship wins, four Premiership wins, seven Regal Trophy honours and five Lancashire Cup wins.

Of course, most of those triumphs – and his finest moments – did not take place at Central Park, but that does not stop the former Wigan St Patricks' amateur having many fond memories of the stadium where he made his name. He rarely had a bad game and it was no wonder fans were stunned when he left Wigan in 1997.

Edwards fondly remembers becoming a world champion in 1987 – who wouldn't? "The Manly game was the first of its kind and the atmosphere, the occasion, was something special," he recalls. "It was a bruising football match played that night under the old five-yard rule – but that game was one of the highlights of my career.

Shaun Edwards in action against Hull in the Regal Trophy.

"Under Graeme Lowe we used to meet up at the ground an hour and a half before the game. We used to meet in the old boardroom and from there you could look out onto the ground. It was 6pm when we got there and the game kicked-off at eight, and already there must have been 15,000 people inside – I thought, "Good God!" By the time the game started

Shaun Edwards pictured with some of the silverware at Central Park in 1996, looking forward to the Premiership Final at Old Trafford. There they beat St Helens 44-14.

I think there were people standing on the toilets!

"When we ran out and all the fireworks went off it was incredible – I have played before crowds of 100,000 people but there was more noise inside Central Park that night. The fans are closer to the pitch and it is so much more intense."

The atmosphere might have been better than that in the national stadium, but the record-breaking run of Challenge Cup wins was extra special all the same. "The Wembley homecomings were always great," Edwards said. "When we did eight in a row I think they just got better and better. None of the fans ever got tired of it – how could you?"

Naturally, one of the moments that sticks in

Shaun Edwards looks to slip one out of the back door. He did, scored two tries, and helped his team to a 78-4 win against Workington on August 24th 1996. It was Wigan's third highest score in the history of the club.

Edwards races clear for another try with only the referee to beat.

Edwards' mind is his first Central Park try, against Castleford on January 8th 1984, a game which the home side won 32-6. He had already played three league games at stand-off and after that introduction he would rarely be out of the side.

He said, "I don't think I scored a better try than my first for the club, which was against Castleford in 1984. I picked the ball up and ran 75 yards – I just ran and ran, and scored between the posts. I wasn't one for scoring individual tries – I was more of a finisher – so I rate that as my best score.

"It was an amazing feeling. The crowd went mad and I went wild as well, and I think I managed to embarrass myself in the process. After that I needed a taxi to get back to the halfway line!"

Like all the homegrown talents the club has nurtured, Edwards was brought up on Central Park.

Going to the school in the shadow of the Popular Stand and learning his craft on pastures next to the stadium made him even closer to the club than most.

"Central Park has played a massive part in my life. I used to go to St Mary's School and when I started playing rugby I trained on the old training field at the ground. When I was about eight or nine I used to sneak into the ground – this was before they had all the security. I knew all the holes in the walls – in fact I think I was the master of sneaking in! I used to spend a lot of time around Scholes and Central Park was always nearby."

His career at Wigan may have ended in 1997, but his influence at Central Park remained until the end.

Edwards beats Roger Simpson of Bradford Northern to score again at Central Park.

There's no one near Edwards as he goes in for another score, to the delight of the Central Park crowd.

Wigan 30 St Helens 2, Lancashire Cup Semi-final, October 2nd 1985

Steve Ella scored a great try after coming off the bench for his debut in the Lancashire Cup semi-final clash at Central Park on October 2nd 1985. The game also gave Ellery Hanley his first taste of derby action.

On their way to winning the Lancashire Cup in 1985, Wigan crushed St Helens as the tide of rugby league power began to switch from Knowsley Road to Central Park. The full extent of this change in power emerged a year later, the 1986-87 season, when Wigan completed their first league-double over the old enemy since 1962.

The cherry and whites had come out of their doldrums in the late 1970s and early 1980s and with a combination of good management, quality overseas imports and talented locals, entered into a decade when they would dominate the game.

The semi-final was the first derby Ellery Hanley played in, but there were tries for Shaun Wane, Greg Dowling, and two for young stand-off Shaun Edwards. Steve Ella came off the bench to score a

wonder try, one of three he scored in four derby appearances for Wigan. David Stephenson kicked five goals.

The attendance at Central Park was 18,544. The following year, again in a Lancashire Cup semi-final, the crowd at Central Park was 28,252 when Wigan beat St Helens 22-16.

It was the start of a new golden era.

Wigan: Hampson, Henley-Smith, Stephenson, Hanley, Whitfield, Edwards, Ford, Dowling, Kiss, Wane, Du Toit, Goodway, Potter. Subs: Ella, Case
St Helens: Loughlin, Ledger, Peters, Veivers, Day, Arkwright, Holding, Burke, Dwyer, Gorley, Forber, Haggerty, Platt. Subs: Litherland, Allen.

David Stephenson punches the air as another try beckons, the Halifax chasers have just about given up catching him.

David Stephenson kicks for goal while Martin Dermott looks on. Stephenson played at centre for Wigan between the 1981-82 and 1987-88 seasons, kicking 286 goals in 209 appearances, and also helping himself to 71 tries.

and guided Wigan back to Wembley in 1985. This time they came away with the trophy, beating Hull 28-24 in a Final that many fans regard as the greatest Challenge Cup Final ever.

Andy Goodway races away to score a try. Goodway, who signed from Oldham, was a hard-running forward and served Wigan from 1985 to 1993.

Nick Du Toit takes the aerial route over the Hull full-back to score a great try. Du Toit came off the bench to score this try, helping Wigan to a 46-12 win in the first round Premiership game on April 28th 1985.

Joe Lydon in full flight. Signed from Widnes in 1985, Lydon was a class act and a great goalkicker.

After coming to Wigan in the 1993-94 season, Va'aiga Tuigamala quickly established himself as a fan's favourite. He was fast, skillful and strong, and always looked happy. Mind you, he won eight medals with Wigan before returning to rugby union with Newcastle Falcons. So he had plenty to smile about.

Andy Gregory spent five years at Wigan and collected 16 trophies in that time. The unmistakable scrum half called all the shots – and not just on the field, either.

Mal Meninga leads the Haka dance for the benefit of those in the Douglas Stand at Central Park, prior to a Great Britain v Australia international.

Big Mal Meninga on the charge for the Aussie tourists with Shaun Edwards in pursuit.

Back at Central Park the covered sprinting track at the rear of the Kop and part of the Colinfield car park disappeared when Central Park Way was built in 1986, and at the start of the 1986-87 season the original cladding around the

Douglas Stand was replaced with cherry and white sheeting.

By 1986 Wigan's all-conquering side was taking shape. New signings included Ellery Hanley, Denis Betts, Dean Bell, Andy Goodway, Brett Kenny and John Ferguson, while Shaun Edwards was now a Wigan 'veteran' at the grand old age of 20!

In October 1986 a new boardroom was built on stilts over the turnstiles on the right

Ellery Cuthwyn Hanley signed from Bradford Northern in 1986 and remained at Wigan until the 1990-91 season. A great all-round player, arguably the best in Wigan's modern history, he won four Challenge Cup medals, three championships, four Lancashire Cup and Regal Trophy/ John Player trophies, one Premiership medal and one World Club champions' medal. He scored 189 tries in 202 starts.

Ellery Hanley scores between the posts, with not a defender in sight.

Aussie winger John Ferguson, who had the knack of beating defenders, in action here against Castleford on February 3rd 1985. He scored four tries in the game, in probably his best performance for the club. He helped Wigan to lift the Challenge Cup that year – scoring the opening try in that game, and in all scored 24 stunning tries in 25 games.

of the pavilion, and new safety legislation meant that during the season the old crush barriers were updated in the Popular Side and the Spion Kop for £50,000. The Kangaroos – an awesome rugby league force by now – were in England on a three-match tour and Australia's interest in the pre-series friendly against Wigan at Central Park was such that Aussie Channel 10 televised the event.

Vice-chairman Maurice Lindsay promised a night like no other at Central Park, and that's what Wigan got. There was a razza-

Dean Bell scores his first try at Central Park, watched by David Stephenson.

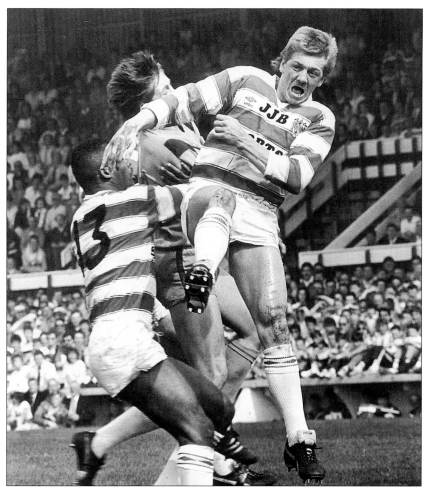

Full-back Steve Hampson in the thick of the action against St Helens on Good Friday, 1987.

matazz opening, complete with live music and parachutists bearing Wigan and Australian flags. In the game itself the cherry and whites gave the Aussies a scare, but lost 26-18 against a side containing Gene Miles, Brett Kenny and Wally Lewis. Over 30,000 people were in Central Park, and in many ways the game was a blueprint for Wigan's famous 'World Club Challenge' against Manly a year later.

In 1986 also the directors had considered extending the Popular stand to the full length of the field at the cost of £500,000, and in

Ellery Hanley is all wrapped up by the Saints defence in this Good Friday derby game from 1987. St Helens couldn't stop him scoring two tries, though, as Wigan won 42-12.

In 1987 Wigan were league champions for the first time in 27 years, and they celebrated in style at Central Park after beating Featherstone Rovers 62-7 on April 5th.

Reminiscent of 1950, eight Wigan players are selected for Great Britain to play against Papua New Guinea in 1987. They are Joe Lydon, Andy Goodway, David Stephenson, Brian Case, Steve Hampson, Shaun Edwards, Ellery Hanley and Andy Gregory.

1988 there were plans to extend each end of the Douglas Stand to include a further 712 seats. Neither schemes ever came to fruition.

In 1987 Wigan won the championship for the first time in 27 years, while they had already won the Lancashire Cup Final for the second year running. They were also John Player winners as well as Premiership championships as the silverware began to mount up. By that time Wigan had eight players in the Great Britain squad.

1989 started with Wigan winning a John Player Trophy semifinal 26-10 against Warrington at Central Park in front of more than 18,000 spectators. Andy Gregory had been dropped from the first team and wanted out, but came on as a substitute for the JPS Final at Burnden Park, Bolton – a game in which Jonathan Davies helped Wigan win. Coach Graham Lowe relented later in the season and Gregory was back in the starting line-up.

Wigan 8 Manly 2 October 7th 1987

This was probably the greatest triumph at Central Park, when Wigan beat Australia's finest and were crowned rugby league world champions.

There were no tries, but the game was as exciting and as tense as any, with defences dominating the natural try-scorers both sides were blessed with. The crowd of 36,895 was only 105 short of the capacity, and the biggest at the ground for 22 years.

It was fitting that Central Park was the venue for the first meeting of the northern and southern hemispheres, and it was largely down to Wigan chairman Maurice Lindsay that the game was played.

Wigan were seeking to end 10 years of Australian domination in the game and, greeted with a fireworks display, they did just that. Fans from all over the world came to see the game, and watched Wigan win courtesy of four penalty kicks from David Stephenson.

The setting for the Wigan v Manly World Club Challenge game in 1987. The fireworks display would not be the only sparks to fly that evening.

A fight breaks out involving Ellery Hanley, Brian Case and Manly's Des Hasler and Dale Shearer, with Phil Daley joining in. Hasler had just stamped on Shaun Wane, so things got a little bit heated. Referee John Holdsworth is about to bring order to the proceedings.

They also saw Manly's hard man Ron Gibbs sent off after 55 minutes for hitting Joe Lydon in the face with his elbow, while Cliff Lyons and Wigan's Brian Case were sin-binned. There were two fights, one between Shaun Edwards and Dale Shearer, and one after Des Hasler stamped on Shaun Wane. It was a game not for the feint-hearted!

Man of the match that evening was second-rower Wane, whose huge defensive display earned him the award. His personal memories of the game are vivid.

"I remember we got to the ground earlier than usual. We all sat in silence in the dressing room and we could hear the buzz of the crowd, people milling around outside the door, and Graham Lowe very cleverly just

The new electronic scoreboard shows just why everybody had spent 80 minutes jostling for a good view!

Henderson Gill is on top of the world, and celebrates with some ecstatic young supporters.

A Manly attack. Shaun Wane's tackle may be in vain but Shaun Edwards is cutting across to cover.

left us to it – just let the atmosphere of the night get to us. And it worked.

"When we got out on the field the fireworks were still going off – there were so many of them there was a smog around the ground. We had cheerleaders who went out with flags, and the noise from the crowd was unbelievable – it was as loud as playing at Wembley when there was 100,000 people there. But it was a better atmosphere, people from my own town.

"The build up to the game had been so different. I remember all the talk was about Manly being champions and what they were going to do to us – all the British press didn't give us much of a chance. Manly were a top team. But I remember by that evening I just couldn't wait to get started, and get in the thick of it.

"The game was very quick and very aggressive. I don't think it was the best game of all time but there was so much riding on it. It was very physical and a few tackles sailed close to the wind, but I think the game had everything – it was aggression pushed to the limit.

"Near the end of the game their prop Phil Daley was taken off with broken ribs. After that their players were staying down after the tackle, and we could see that we had them. It was a fantastic feeling. We knew they had come from the other side of the world as heavy favourites, and we had battered them.

"People had said at the time that English players did not have the bottle to play an intense game of rugby, but we did it for 80 minutes.

"I know I played all right – I don't know how many tackles I put in – but I thought there were quite a few guys in our pack who could have won man of the match. I was very pleased about it but it was a great performance from the Wigan pack.

"When the hooter went it's hard to describe how I felt. It was as though my body was jumping out of my skin, such was the excitement. It was unbelievable.

"We did a few laps of honour with the trophy afterwards then when we got back into the dressing room everybody was going wild. The press were there and they got showered in champagne.

Then the whole team went to Kilhey Court where we gently let our hair down!

"After the game I never slept a wink and I got up the next day and still didn't feel tired. We trained the next day, like a loosening-up session, but we were still on a high because what we had done was such a massive achievement. It meant so much."

The teams on that historic evening were:

Wigan: Hampson, Russell, Stephenson, Lydon, Gill, Edwards, Gregory, Case(Lucas), Kiss, Wane, Goodway, Potter, Hanley. Subs: Byrne, Gildart, West

Manly: Shearer, Ronson, Williams, O'Connor, Davis, Lyons, Hasler, Daley, Cochrane, Gately, Gibbs, Cunningham(Shaw), Vautin. Subs: Brokenshire, Ticehurst, Pocock.

All hell breaks loose in the dressing room after the match as Graham Lowe and his charges celebrate in grand fashion. Even the reporters were drowned in champagne.

The last scoreboard at Central Park. It was installed in January 1989, replacing a similar but smaller board, then moved to the corner at Hilton Street when the Whitbread Stand was built. Here it shows Wigan scoring a point a minute in the first half against Bradford.

A view of Central Park from referee John Holdsworth

John Holdsworth made the leap from Grade Two to Grade One status for the 1980-1981 season, just in time to see Wigan get back from Division Two to Division One – and the start of their revival.

At Grade One, Leeds-based John was able to referee first grade games as well as A-team games and first went to Central Park for a first team fixture against York on March 7th 1982.

"I can't remember the score, but I remember the feeling," he said. "It was brilliant and I loved every minute of it. At that time every time I did a big game it was another feather in my cap, and there was no better place than Central Park.

"I was lucky, I think, because the club started going places when they came up out of Division Two and the crowds just got bigger and bigger. The minimum was 10,000 and for the big derby games against St Helens and Warrington there were 16 and 17,000. There was a great buzz around the ground and I think it's always better to referee in front of big crowds. It gives you that extra edge, that great awareness – you are more keyed-up."

Like all refs, he was never able to please everybody and he admitted it was a 'miracle' if a certain local newspaper gave him a rating as high as seven out of 10!

He has no doubt as to his favourite Central Park games in which he was the man in the middle. John was the man who sent off Ron 'Rambo' Gibbs in the 1987 Manly game – a match he reckons was better to be a part of than any Challenge Cup Final at Wembley.

"I'd done the St Helens versus Halifax Cup Final at Wembley that year," he recalled, "the first to get

He was tough and took no nonsense from anyone – and Kelvin Skerrett was a hard man, too. John Holdsworth lays down the law during the Boxing Day derby in 1993.

gate receipts of over £1 million. There must have been 60,000 more people at Wembley than at Central Park yet the atmosphere for that Manly game was far better.

"I used to come to Wigan on the M61 and come off near Horwich, down Dicconson Lane. The traffic was already backed-up to the traffic lights and it was only half-past five! The game didn't kick-off until eight o'clock. For a while I was really worried I might be late.

"In terms of personal achievement that game will always stay in my mind. The crowd was breathtaking. I remember send-

John Holdsworth keeps pace with Shaun Edwards in Wigan's game against Leeds at Central Park on September 10th 1993.

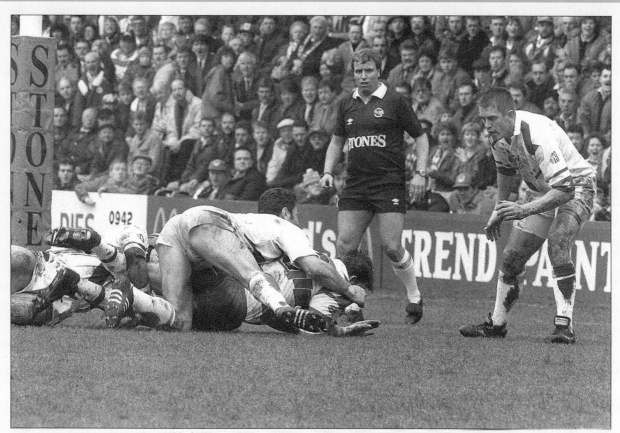

John Holdsworth declares the tackle is completed in Wigan's Good Friday game against Saints in 1993.

ing Gibbs off for following through. Joe Lydon had gone for a drop goal but the next thing I knew he was on the floor. I had a gut feeling about what happened but the touch judge came on and said Gibbs had followed through with his elbow. I said, 'Are you sure?' He said yes so I turned to Gibbs and said, 'Off you go.'

"I remember Manly came closest to scoring and they even got over the line, but the man was definitely held up over the line. He was on his back. The

Referee John Holdsworth watches Frano Botica kick at goal during a league game against Bradford Northern on April 15th 1994.

Manly players claimed they'd scored afterwards, but you always get that.

"One of the other great games I refereed was when Wigan drew 16-all with St Helens (Challenge Cup fourth round, 1995). That was pretty dramatic. I spoke to the groundsman Taffy (Derek Jones) before the game because when I got there the pitch was virtually under water! It was a TV game but it was so close to being called-off – I finished up helping the ground staff to fork the pitch."

John has blown the whistle on a peculiar habit one of the Wigan players had during his duties at Central Park. "There was a fad at Wigan concerning Joe Lydon," he explained. "For some reason he always used the referee's toilet – never the players'. I could almost guarantee that 30 minutes before kick-off there would be a knock at the door, and I'd say, 'That's Joe Lydon.' And it was.

"He'd stand there and ask if he could use the toilet. What am I going to say? No? I asked him once why he used the ref's and he just said, 'I like it in here.'"

That year the players' tunnel was covered after a visiting team's coach had a beer thrown over him, and a new electronic scoreboard with a larger display was installed. Wigan also hoped to sell the training pitch and car park to City Grove for £2,500,000 – later reduced to £1,800,000 – and use the money to build a new Popular Side stand. But City Grove's plans to use the land as a garden centre, DIY store and fast-food restaurant were rejected by planners and the whole deal fell through.

That disappointment was put aside a few weeks later when plans were approved for a new cantilever stand at the Pavilion end that would become known as the Whitbread Stand. The plans included installing 1,840 seats, a row of executive boxes, hospitality areas, an extension to the Riverside Club and a new pub for supporters, the Central Park Tavern. The pub plans were abandoned and the discovery of mine workings in the foundations meant building was delayed and costs escalated. The revamped Riverside Club opened in February 1991 but the stand did not open until the following season.

The directors were unhappy that spectators at one end of the stand had a limited view of the pitch, and a 200-seat extension was added to the stand. A police room,

Wigan's training ground at the rear of the Spion Kop – nothing special, perhaps, but always a part of Central Park. In 1992 it was earmarked for a housing development but the plans never went through.

John Monie watches his team's performance from the 'extended' eagles' nest, built into the roof of the Douglas tand.

public address room and two extra executive boxes were also provided, and the stand was first used on September 8th 1991 when Wigan beat Widnes 26-18.

When the Whitbread stand was built the pavilion structure all but disappeared but brick supports with memorial stones for Jim Leytham, Bert Jenkins, Charlie Seeling and Johnny Thomas remained. The stand was the last major development at Central Park.

The 1990s began as the 1980s had ended, with Wigan winning everything. John Monie enjoyed a clean sweep in his four years at the club after Graham Lowe had got Wigan used to success. The talented players kept on coming – Martin Offiah, Andy Farrell, Frano

The building of the Whitbread Stand in 1991, the last major construction to take place at Central Park.

The building of the Whitbread Stand, and the final disappearing act of the original pavilion building that had stood on the site since 1909.

The building of the Whitbread Stand, which would have 2,000 seats, executive boxes, hospitality areas, and an extension to the Riverside Club.

The Whitbread Stand before it was extended. Some seats on the far left in this picture had obstrcuted views of the pitch, so the seating was extended and the side panel moved along.

The Whitbread Stand – latterly named the Billy Boston Stand – and the forecourt as it was in the ground's final years.

A familiar view to thousands of Wigan fans. There is the bridge that many crossed to get to the ground, and the doorways through which hundreds would queue for tickets.

Maurice Lindsay

Here is Maurice Lindsay, third from left, together with fellow Wigan directors Jack Hilton, Tom Rathbone, and Jack Robinson.

Maurice Lindsay has a long association with Wigan rugby league. It started when he was a boy and supporter when he cheered from the terraces, and ended as the chairman in the boardroom of that same club. His first memory was of a game when Wigan lost to Oldham at Central Park in the 1950s. Some of his last, 40 years later, were of winning every competition in the game and in becoming world champions in a tournament he helped to create.

Lindsay, a former plant-hire contractor and occasional bookmaker, joined the board of directors in 1979 and in 1982 he, along with Jack Robinson, Tom Rathbone and chairman Jack Hilton, formed a new board. Their aim was to put the club back on the map after suffering the ignominy of relegation in 1980. Not only did they help bounce the club back into Division One, they created the greatest rugby league dynasty the game has seen – and probably ever will see.

The Wigan team of the early 1950s was also stuffed with great players, and this period marked the beginning of Lindsay's affinity towards the club.

He said: "I was living in Horwich at the time and I went to a boy's Catholic school – about 160 of us used to travel on the train. That's when I met Wigan enthusiasts who all told me I had to go to Central Park, because they were playing Oldham who were fantastic.

"I was 12 years old on my first ever visit. I remember catching the number 16 bus from Horwich, got off at the top of Greenough Street and walked down with all these big fans. There were about 30,000 people there that day and I stood on the terraces in awe.

"I got confused, though. Oldham were playing in their cherry and white hoop shirts and Wigan were in blue, and I watched this brilliant team in cherry and white and thought it was Wigan. Then I realised it wasn't, and Wigan had been beaten. That surprised me because I thought Wigan were a top team.

"When I went back to school there were kids from Oldham there – it was a posh school – and they were taunting us. So I decided to stick up for Wigan."

So in 1979, Maurice Lindsay's business dealings with the club led him to become involved in running the affairs at Central Park. Wigan's fortunes on the field were in free-fall and the directors came to him for help.

Lindsay said: "I was excited, but at the first meeting I found out the club had no money and the cheques were not going through the bank. So I rolled up my sleeves and got stuck in.

"While I was on the board we went through many fantastic periods and moments you will never forget. Since I left Wigan things have never been quite as enjoyable – in my capacity now I have to rise above the emotion. I feel as though my blood is in Central Park and I am more comfortable with that."

Lindsay undoubtedly has thousands of fond memories at Central Park, but three principal events symbolise them all. Wigan's league triumph in 1987, the first for 27 years, was remarkable. They won 28 out of 30 matches, finished with a 15-point winning margin over second-placed St Helens, scored a record 174 tries and conceded

just 29. Only Warrington had the better of them.

Wigan secured the title two weeks before the end of the season with a thumping 62-7 win against Featherstone. The game is among Lindsay's favourite Central Park moments.

"We just killed everybody that year," he recalled, "and that really was the beginning of a new era. There was such a buzz around the ground because everyone knew it was our title. We made an announcement to the people not to invade the pitch at the end of the game so the lads could do a proper lap of honour. Nobody did. It was a wonderful occasion and it really told me what a great town Wigan is."

Maurice and Ellery Hanley in the Central Park tunnel. It looks like Wigan have won again.

There is one game which keeps cropping up in these pages, but it is both unsurprising and worthy of such repetition. The Manly game was Lindsay's brainchild, a means of making Australia take notice of the Wigan club and providing an early season glamour game. Getting the game on was not all plain sailing, but there was no doubting its success.

Lindsay remembers the night as well as any other die-hard fan, but has a more unusual tale to tell. "We had just got the new boardroom at the Pavilion end and they were still painting it at 5.15pm – we were kicking-off against Manly at eight o'clock. It was still being painted when the Manly directors walked up the steps. And you could smell it all night. We had to tell people not to lean on the bar or they would take the varnish off.

"That was the last time Central Park was crammed to the rafters – at least in the days before all the safety laws came into play. People were even climbing the electricity pylons. And the great thing about that game is all the Wigan players on the field that night were English. It was localised and that made it all the more marvellous.

"My other great memory is actually of a week, at the end of 1991. We had played and had been successful in every Cup competition and we had to win four games in six days to win the league.

"We had just beaten St Helens. Then on the Sunday we played against Castleford at Central Park in front of 22,000 fans, then on Tuesday we had to play Widnes and there were nearly 30,000 there for that. Then on Thursday we had to play Bradford and

18,500 were there for that one. We were losing that one 18-2, were tired and had injuries, but Ellery Hanley – what a football player! He was brilliant and we fought back to 18-all. Frano Botica tried a drop goal near the end of the game that would have won it for us.

"In four days we had 70,000 people go through the turnstiles at Central Park. The staff worked night and day, non-stop. John Monie was his calm and collected self, but there were people everywhere, coming in for tickets and all excited. The town was in a frenzied state.

"Then we had to go to Leeds on Saturday. We won that and won the title. I think it's fair to say that week will live with me for the rest of my life."

As much as the ground, Lindsay remembers the supporters who packed the terraces for every home game. Yet their involvement with Central Park never stopped there.

Lindsay recalled, "I remember waking up one Sunday, looking out and seeing everywhere covered

in snow. I think we were due to play Warrington at Central Park that day. I went down to the ground with Arthur Stone and Jack Robinson and the pitch was white all over, and there was no way we could clear it ourselves. So we put a call out on the local radio for supporters to come down to the ground and help us clear the snow. The message was clearly 'bring a shovel.'

"I have a vivid memory of this. We had about 300 people down there, all armed with brushes and shovels, and we cleared the snow and the game went ahead. There were 16,000 people there for the game. But I had to pause to see some 300 people, fathers, mothers and children helping to clear their beloved Central Park. It was amazing.

"But that is what Central Park was all about. It was about the ground and the people who went there to see a great team play."

Maurice Lindsay strikes a familiar pose at Central Park. So, too, come to think of it, does the Challenge Cup.

Wigan director Jack Robinson announces the signing of Frano Botica. Coach John Monie wasn't convinced he was a good buy at first, but in the end Robinson was proved right.

Sam Panapa charges for the try-line, with Martin Offiah helpfully pointing him in the right direction.

Billy McGinty holds aloft the championship trophy in 1992 in front of an ecstatic Popular Stand. Wigan clinched the championship with two league games to spare, having beaten Bradford 50-8 at Central Park.

Kelvin Skerrett nails Andrew Gee, with a helping hand from Phil Clarke, in the 1992 World Club Challenge match against Brisbane Broncos on October 30th at Central Park. Despite his efforts Wigan lose the game – and their world champions crown.

Denis Betts is caught on the ankle by Allan Langer. A total of 17,746 spectators saw Wigan lose the 1992 World Club match against Brisbane 22-8.

Joe Lydon puts up some resistance aginst the old enemy, St Helens, during the 1993 Good Friday clash. Lydon could play anywhere in the back line and he had a good kicking game.

Shaun Edwards and Martin Offiah show off the championship trophy for the 1992-93 season. Wigan finished the season level on points with St Helens but clinched the trophy thanks to a better points difference – the first time the Division One champions had been decided in such a way.

John Dorahy came from Newcastle Knights to coach Wigan in June 1993, and John Monie was a hard act to follow. Wigan lost the Regal Trophy Final to Castleford, but they won Division One and the Challenge Cup against Leeds. Two days later Dorahy was sacked after he and chairman Jack Robinson had a bust-up on the team coach travelling back from Wembley.

Botica, Jason Robinson and Va'aiga Tuigamala – and so did the trophies. Offiah admitted that the fear of losing was their main motivation for winning!

In the 1994-95 season the idea of leaving Central Park and moving to a new stadium at Robin Park first surfaced. The club thought they could move to a new facility in conjunction with Wigan Council but local businessman and millionaire Dave Whelan was reportedly offering finance to develop

Wiganers have always known to queue along the River Douglas for tickets. Here the cherry and white faithful are hoping to get their seats for Wembley.

Wigan 74 Leeds 6
Premiership Semi-final, May 10th 1992

Martin Offiah races in for one of his 10 tries against Leeds in a Premiership semi-final on May 10th 1992. After the game Maurice Lindsay was almost lost for words – but not quite. He said: "I was brought up in the great days of the legendary Billy Boston – but now we have entered a new era with Martin Offiah."

Leaving a desperate Carl Gibson in his wake, Offiah streaks in for his seventh try. "He's the fastest animal I've ever seen on two legs." said Gene Miles.

JUST over a week after Martin Offiah had been denied a Challenge Cup Final hat-trick at Wembley, the winger made up for it at Central Park by scoring a record 10 tries against Leeds.

It was difficult to keep count, but 'Chariots' touched down on seven, 23, 27, 35, 40, 45, 56, 60, 63 and 67 minutes, and for every one try scored, Leeds' coach and former Wiganer Doug Laughton chain-smoked another three cigarettes!

The 18,286 crowd sat enthralled as Wigan ripped big-spenders Leeds apart. The cherry-and-white army taunted: "Are you watching Ellery?" as Hanley had moved across the Pennines – but sat out this particular game because of injury.

Offiah fell one try short of the all-time match record but beat Wigan's previous best, seven touchdowns, shared by Johnny Ring, Gordon Ratcliffe, Billy Boston and Green Vigo.

Following the game he told The *Wigan Observer*, "After the disappointment of missing out on an hat-trick at Wembley, to finish up with 10 tries in one afternoon is unbelievable. I would have been quite happy with a hat-trick.

It just keeps on getting better – Offiah is congratulated by Billy McGinty and Denis Betts after another score against Leeds.

Martin Offiah acknowledges the cheers of the crowd after his 10-try feat against Leeds. Leeds skipper Garry Schofield said: "He may be a winger but he pops up everywhere. He is the greatest."

"I didn't realise until Keith Mills told me at half time that I was within two of equalling the Wigan club record. But anything is possible with this team. They are the best in the world."

Later that year Shaun Edwards equalled the record with 10 against Swinton in a Lancashire Cup second round match. But as far as Central Park was concerned, Offiah's feat would never be matched.

The other try scorers that day were skipper Dean Bell with two, and Martin Dermott and David Myers with one each. Frano Botica slotted the ball between the sticks nine times, and Wigan won 74-6.

Wearing a Leeds jersey that day, though wanting to forget it, was former Wigan front row man Shaun Wane. "It was the worst day of my life – well, the worst 80 minutes," he recalled. "I just kept watching Martin Offiah go by.

"When it got to about 58-0 we had head and feed at the scrum, and we even lost that. I could hear Andy Platt giggling to himself while I was coming out with a load of swear words. It was awful, a game I couldn't wait to finish. I'm a bad loser so that didn't help."

Wigan: Hampson, Lydon, Bell, Miles, Offiah, Botica, Edwards, Cowie, Dermott, Platt, Betts, McGinty Clarke.

Leeds: Ford, Deakin, Edwards, Gibson, Fawcett, Innes, Goulding, Molloy, Maskill, Wane, Divorty, Dixon, Schofield.

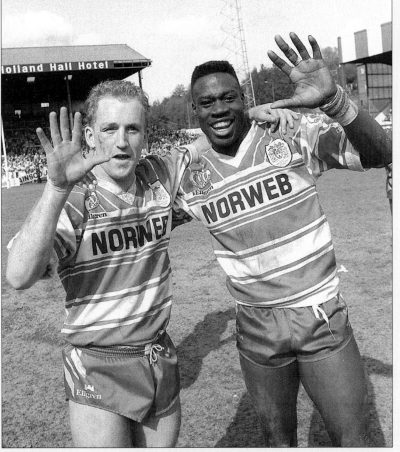

Martin Offiah celebrates with Shaun Edwards after his 10 tries against Leeds. This picture proved to be prophetic since Edwards helped himself to 10 tries at Station Road four months later.

Central Park in return for some control of the club. Wigan rugby believed they could go it alone, using grants and National Lottery money, together with the proceeds from their sale of Central Park, to build a new stadium. But it soon emerged that the club would be required to share with Wigan Athletic.

At the annual general meeting in March 1995, chairman Jack Robinson told shareholders that the club would never ground-share with Latics, and although further discussions were held in 1996 about a Robin Park stadium they eventually ran out of steam with no decision made.

On the rugby field things were more clear-cut. By 1995 Wigan had won eight Challenge Cups in a row, an incredible achievement, and there were no signs that the team could be stopped. For eight years the club dominated rugby league – no other sport had ever seen such a hold on its rivals – yet the town of Wigan never once tired of it. Year after year the supporters would lap it up on Wembley Way and then cheer as the trophy made its way back to Central Park.

Andy Farrell

Andrew Farrell was described as a 'teenage sensation' when he burst onto the scene in October 1991. Signed from Orrell St James, the 16-year-old was used as an effective substitute during the 1992-1993 season but it was in 1994 that he became a fully established first team player, usually occupying the second row.

But Farrell's first association with Central Park was as a fan, and he was a regular, excited youngster in the hen pen. He said: "I remember sitting on the front wall all the time watching the games – and one of the best memories I have is of the Wigan versus Manly game. It was chock-a-block. I remember getting there for half past three and the game didn't start

Andy Farrell burst onto the Wigan scene in 1991 after signing from Orrell St James. He made his debut as a 16-year-old against Keighley that year, and since then he has gone on to skipper both Wigan and Great Britain. Farrell is a strong runner, fine play-maker and a great goalkicker. He is marching up Wigan's list of prolific points scorers – but he still has his work cut out if he is going to catch Jim Sullivan! He is seen here shaping for goal against Sheffield Eagles in 1996.

until 8pm. That was a fantastic night. I remember looking over the wall and watching the players come out of the tunnel, when the tunnel was uncovered."

John Monie handed Farrell his first team debut on November 24th 1991 when Wigan played Keighley in the second round of the Regal Trophy. Farrell was a substitute for Mike Forshaw and although another debutant, Stuart Turner, was the talk of the fans following the game after scoring a hat-trick, Monie recognised Farrell's potential straightaway.

"Playing for Wigan at Central Park was a dream come true," Farrell said. "They used to play the Gladiators song as was the Wigan tradition and coming out to that and the noise was fantastic. I remember I wasn't that nervous because I had already been training there. But the aura of the place is wonderful, when you first go out and look around. After a few years you tend to take it for granted but when you do it for the first time it catches your breath."

Farrell won the man of the match award in Wigan's 8-8 draw against St Helens on April 9th 1993 in front of 29,839 people at Central Park – one of his best memories.

"It was the first derby game I had been involved in and it was only my third or fourth match. I came on as a sub after 15 minutes and I ended up getting the man of the match award. I was still only 17 years old so it was a bit special.

"All the derby games were tremendous. We would get crowds of 28,000 and you couldn't hear yourself think. Everybody talks about Wembley but it was not like Central Park when there was a big crowd. The atmosphere was special.

"Some of the best days at Central Park were when we used to come back from Wembley. The changing rooms used to get done up every year. When we'd come back we'd rip the coat pegs off, just messing about – I know that sounds mad. It is those sort of days that you miss – and I don't think they will let us do that kind of thing at the new stadium!"

Farrell made seven more substitute appearances before starting in the second row in a 27-14 win at Warrington on April 12th 1993, when he scored a try. His first try at Central Park was against Leigh on October 19th that year by which time he was a reg-

Andy Farrell breaks free of the tackle against St Helens, Good Friday 1993.

Andy Farrell causing havoc against Saints in the same game.

ular starter in the side. Frano Botica was the kicker and Shaun Edwards the skipper at the time. In 1994 he was a try-scorer and goalkicker for Great Britain and was also successful in the under 21s side.

But he really came of age in the 1994-95 season when he kicked 60 goals and scored five tries in his 32 starts. Now captain, inspiration and chief goal-kicker in the side, Farrell recognises how important Central Park was to the town, and is pleased that he played a major part in its closing chapters.

He said: "Central Park means an awful lot – whenever people talk about Wigan rugby they talk about Central Park. It's a massive part of the town's history. If you talk to the loyal Wigan fans they will actually call it heaven – that's the word they will use because it means so much to them.

"Central Park will be missed all over the world. All the Aussie players want to play there – the Gateshead players are glad they did it, and I know

Andy Farrell on the charge in his debut game at Central Park in 1991.

Greg Florimo and Mark Reber are glad that they came in time to play there. It is that important.

"I am very proud to have competed there. The place will go down in history as the most remembered ground and people will still be talking about it 100 years from now. Wigan is such a special place for rugby league and within that Central Park is even more special."

Wiganers know Wembley better than anyone, and many can't break the habit – they go every year whether Wigan are in the Final or not.

Super League arrived, and the game was about to say goodbye to winter rugby. Snow-covered pitches and covers were to become a thing of the past at Central Park and ice-cream stalls would now stand alongside the hot-pie kiosks.

Wigan Rugby League Club became Wigan Warriors, though the lettering on the Whitbread Stand would never subscribe to the whims of the Super League masterminds. While many people crit-

Remember the joys of winter rugby? Assistant groundsman Billy Arnold is concerned that Wigan's first Challenge Cup game of 1996 might not go ahead because of frost.

Super League meant summer rugby, and summer rugby meant fans wanted ice cream instead of hot meat pies at half-time.

Groundsman Derek Jones, better known as Taffy, thinks it is unlikely the rugby match will go ahead.

icised the revolution the clubs simply got on with it, but at Wigan warm-weather rugby was not the only change. They also stopped winning, and started losing some of their best players.

Plans to upgrade the ground were forgotten as the need to improve on the pitch became paramount. In 1996 Wigan were dumped out of the Challenge Cup at an early stage, they lost ground in the league and attendances began to fall. Problems snowballed into 1997 when the situation became critical financially.

Something had to go so the club could stay on an even keel – nothing was too important to prevent its survival.

Central Park was sold. The players, caught in the middle of the uproar, struggled through 1997 as thousands of disillusioned fans

Martin Offiah celebrates his first try in Wigan's 50-6 demolition of Sheffield Eagleson May 29th 1996. He went on to score a hat-trick in that match, and they proved to be the last tries he scored at Central Park in a cherry and white jersey. Later that year Offiah signed a joint deal with London Broncos and Bedford RU.

Scott Quinnell, a Welsh RU forward, took a long time to take to rugby league but when he did he attracted great reviews. His career at Wigan was shortlived, however, as Richmond were able to offer him more money than Wigan could afford. He left in April 1996.

stayed away or protested from the terraces. When the future home of the club was established at the end of that season, Wigan were only too glad to have put the year behind them. Whether it was John Monie's influence the following year, or whether Wigan were just bouncing back to something like normal service, 1998 gave the club its first Super League success.

Wigan won the inaugural Grand

Jason Robinson cuts through London Broncos' defence to score another great try, this one in an 18-all draw on June 9th 1996.

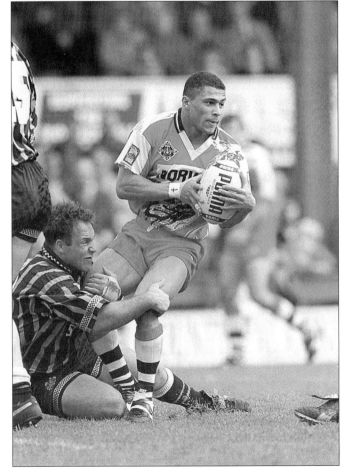

Billy Boston and Tom Van Vollenhoven share a joke as they lead out the teams for the Wigan and St Helens clash at Central Park, on June 21st 1996. Wigan won 35-19 in front of Central Park's record Super League attendance, 20,429.

Wigan full-back Kris Radlinski in action in the Premiership semi-final on September 21st 1997. Wigan beat Sheffield Eagles 22-10 before defeating St Helens 33-20 in the Final.

Jason Robinson, looking for support in Wigan's game against Oldham Bears on April 27th 1997. Robinson signed from Hunslet Boys in 1993 and made his debut as a 19-year-old. That same season he was named Young Player of the Year.

Wigan's Kiwi stand-off Henry Paul splits the Sheffield Eagles defence on August 16th 1998 to score the opening try at Central Park. Wigan won 44-6 on their way to winning the inugural Grand Final at Old Trafford.

In November 1997 John Monie was back at the helm in Wigan. Could he repeat the all-conquering success he achieved with the club during his previous four-year stay?

Final at Old Trafford on October 24th, beating a tough Leeds side 10-4. Wigan had a Challenge Cup homecoming earlier in the season – ending runners-up to the rank outsiders Sheffield Eagles – but decided not to put on a Grand Final bash at Central Park.

Central Park under the floodlights.

The last season at Central Park was not the best. Indifferent form and some poor crowds sometimes gave the impression of a club just whiling away the last months before a move to a new home. But there has been more than enough success and happy times at the ground. And the legacy of Central Park will be very difficult to live up to.

The only piece of Central Park that supporters don't mind being bulldozed. This message has been carved into the terraces.

Love him or loathe him, Gordon 'Golden Gamble' Harrison made the half-time interval at Central Park go so much quicker – and somebody always got a load of money at the end of it. Will there be room for 'Flash' at the JJB Stadium?

Central Park as it was in its final years. This shot was taken on July 28th 1997 when Wigan beat the Canterbury Bulldogs 31-24 in the World Club Challenge.

Central Park from the air.

A free view of the game at the bridge over the River Douglas at Central Park during a Good Friday clash with St Helens.

A fan's view of Central Park — Bill McCormick

Bill McCormick, who has been watching Wigan at Central Park for 75 years, is pictured before the game against Gateshead on Sunday May 9th 1999.

When Bill McCormick was eight years old his aunties clubbed together to buy him a season ticket for Central Park. It cost 7s 6d. A month previously Wigan had staged their first Challenge Cup homecoming and Bill, among the thousands of fans that greeted them, was immediately hooked. It was 1924.

"My aunties used to take me," he said. "I was that little they had to lift me over the turnstiles. We used to go in the Whelley end when they only had shelters. It was wonderful.

"I used to live in one of the houses in Westminster Street on the other side of the River Douglas and the ground was a stone's throw away. When one of my uncles couldn't afford to go he would stand in his bedroom and could see half the ground from the window. I've lived in Whelley for 30 years now and it's the furthest I've ever lived away from the ground."

Bill has supported Wigan for 75 years and has seen most home games. He has missed only one Challenge Cup Final involving Wigan – the famous win over Dewsbury at Wembley in 1929 – but only because he was 13 years old and at that time he couldn't afford to go.

"One of my friends had a wireless set and about eight or 10 people crowded into his house to listen to it. I remember the homecoming, though. There were thousands of people outside the station, past the town hall and all the way to Central Park."

Bill has seen all the great stars in action, from Jim Sullivan to Johnny Ring, Brian Nordgren to Ces Mountford, Billy Boston to Eric Ashton, yet he believes the Wigan team of the late 1980s and early 1990s was the best to grace the field at Central Park.

"Sullivan was a big, good player. The best goal-kicker the club has had. That title's between him and

Frano Botica, but he was better than Frano. It was a different game then, of course. The ball was leather and it got very heavy, but Sullivan was a great goal-kicker – he made it look easy.

"One man that stands out in my mind was the loose forward Jack Price, though I know a few people might wonder why. We signed him from Broughton Rangers. Games were very close in those days but Price was brilliant. He used to run a lot with the ball and that was unusual – it was exciting to watch.

"I went to see Boston for his first game – he was the best winger I have ever seen. There were 8,000 at Central Park for the A-team match – he played centre then, and his first try was nothing really. But his second was a Billy special. He got the ball from near the half way line and weaved his way through the defence. I remember everyone said, "He'll do for this club.""

"I always said he made Eric Ashton. Ashton was a good centre but the defenders always went to Billy because they were worried about what he could do with the ball. That gave Ashton more room. Brian Nordgren was a great winger, and I thought he was the only person who could hold his own against Brian Bevan.

"But the team from 1987 to 1995 is the best rugby team I have ever seen. They had everything as a unit and no one could stop them – I have seen some good teams at Central Park but they were the best. Ellery Hanley was the best of the lot – he could play any-where."

Bill, now 83, will miss Central Park as much as anyone. Having lived so close to it for so long the ground has played a major part in his life.

"I remember during the strikes in 1926 my moth-er used to send me to the club with a bucket and I had to ask the coach Tommy McCarty if I could go on the Spion Kop and pinch some coal. It was just an embankment then, made up of coal and cinders. They used to let me on.

"I've stood in the hen-pen. That was noisy and always full of youngsters, but they always behaved themselves. You booed the ref like everyone else did, of course!

"I'll always remember the St Helens games. The one with the record crowd was good. It was a sunny day, I came on the bus and I had a ticket for the Popular Stand. But I couldn't get anywhere near my seat because there were people everywhere – they were standing at the back and you couldn't get through. So I stood at the back with them.

"I'll miss Central Park. It's always been close to me. I've made a lot of friends at the ground, and had some great times there."

Homecomings

The trophy that had an unbroken eight-year love affair with Central Park's silverware cabinet. It is, of course, the Challenge Cup, here wearing Silk Cut's sponsorship ribbons.

1924
Wigan 21 Oldham 4
Saturday April 12th

The homecoming was a low-key affair, even though Wigan won the Challenge Cup for the first time in their history. The Final was held at Rochdale Hornet's Athletic Ground and 41,831 spectators – a new competition record – watched the game. Wigan were inundated with messages of congratulations from places as far afield as Hull, Oldham and Huddersfield following the win. The trophy was proudly displayed in a luncheon at The Royal Hotel with Wigan Rugby Club, Wigan Borough Football Club and Everton Football Club attending. Later the same week the supporter's club held a whist drive at Empress Hall to celebrate the club's success.

Final team: Sullivan, Ring, Howley, Parker, Van Heerden, Jerram, Hurcombe, Webster, Banks, Van Rooyen, Brown, Roffey, Price.

THIS book has not concerned itself with many of Wigan's triumphs away from Central Park – notably the Challenge Cup wins at Wembley – but for every trip to the famous ground there has been a homecoming equally memorable.

In earlier years the team would return by train and then the bus would take them through packed streets in Wigan town centre, via the town hall, to Central Park. In later triumphs the open-top bus would start at Marus Bridge and bring the town to a standstill as the cavalcade rolled towards Hilton Street.

1929
Wigan 13 Dewsbury 2
Saturday May 4th

The first Final to be held at the Empire Stadium – as it was known then. 'There were wild scenes of

enthusiasm in the town,' the *Wigan Observer* reported, as 30,000 fans waited at the railway station for the team to return. Standishgate, Wallgate and Market Place were packed, and although a civic reception had been arranged to take place at the Town Hall the mayor met the players at the station. A bus then took the team and the Cup to Central Park where Ince All Blacks and Bickershaw Hornets met in the Laing Cup Final. More than 6,000 saw the game, though many were most interested in seeing the Challenge Cup on display.
Final team: Sullivan, Ring, Parker, Kinnear, Brown, Binks, Abram, Hodder, Bennett, Beetham, Stephens, Mason, Sherrington.

1948
Wigan 8
Bradford Northern 3
Saturday May 1st

If you thought the 1989 homecoming was special, picture this: More than 100,000 turned out for the 1948 homecoming – 15,000 more than the population of Wigan!

There were fans lined on the railway embankments from Warrington to Wigan as the train made the final leg of its journey to Wigan North West station. Thousands of people followed the coach along Wallgate and two spectators pushed leather wallets through a coach window as gifts to Ken Gee and Frank Barton. The coach toured Highfield, Poolstock and Worsley Mesnes before return-

ing to the Town Hall where captain Joe Egan held the Cup aloft. After the reception the coach drove round Scholes and Whelley before 5,000 fans greeted the team at Central Park
Final team: Ryan, Ratcliffe, Ward, Ashcroft, Hilton, Mountford, Bradshaw, Gee, Egan, Barton, White, Blan, Hudson.

1951
Wigan 10 Barrow 0
Saturday May 5th

Jimmy Connolly's New Empress Dance Orchestra played *Entry of the Gladiators* when captain Cecil Mountford held the trophy aloft at Wigan North Western railway station – and 15,000 people cheered. Brian Nordgren was missing from the party but it was later revealed he suffered an injury during the match, then had a bad reaction to treatment and was sent home to rest. The coach then toured the town with Lance Todd winner Mountford standing through the sun roof and holding the trophy for all to see.
Final team: Cunliffe, Hilton, Broome, Roughley, Nordgren, Mountford, Bradshaw, Gee, Curran, Barton, Silcock, Slevin, Blan.

1958
Wigan 13
Workington Town 9
Saturday May 10th

More than 60,000 fans lined a nine-mile route around the town when the class of '58 brought home the Challenge Cup. Jack Cunliffe brought the trophy off the train but four players had no time to celebrate with their team-mates. Eric Ashton, Dave Bolton, Mick Sullivan and Brian McTigue stayed in London to board a plane as members of the Great Britain tourist side bound for Australia. Billy Boston had a scare at the Town Hall when he was told his 21-month-old daughter Christina had burned herself and he rushed home, but the accident did not turn out to be serious. At Central Park it took the players half an hour to get from the coach to the pavilion because of the crowds!
Final team: Cunliffe, O'Grady, Ashton, Boston, Sullivan, Bolton, Thomas, Barton, Sayer, McTigue, Cherrington, Collier, McGurrin.

1959
Wigan 30 Hull 13
Saturday May 9th

Fans braved a thunderstorm to welcome home the first team to win successive rugby league Cup Finals at Wembley. Thousands packed the town centre streets and gathered round the Town Hall. Eric Ashton missed out on the homecoming the previous year but he was delighted to be part of the celebrations this time round. "I have never known anything like it," he said at the civic reception. After the formalities the coach continued on to Central Park where the players enjoyed a champagne reception.

Eric Ashton and Mick Sullivan with the Challenge Cup, won for the second successive year back in 1959. Wigan beat Hull 30-13.

The 1965 Wembley Homecoming. The team boarded the coach at Wigan North West station and drove through the town centre.

Final team: Griffiths, Boston, Ashton, Holden, Sullivan, Bolton, Thomas, Bretherton, Sayer, Barton, Cherrington, McTigue, Evans.

North Western station in the early evening and there they boarded a bus and travelled along Wallgate, Library Street and Rodney Street to the Town Hall for a civic reception.

The bus then did an incredible route that took in Poolstock, Pemberton, Beech Hill, Lower Ince, Higher Ince, finally arriving at Central Park an hour after leaving the Town Hall! It was worth taking the scenic route, though, for the fans turned out in their thousands to greet them.

1965
Wigan 20 Hunslet 16
Saturday May 8th

This was the first year Wigan travelled home on Sunday rather than Monday. They arrived at Wigan

The Challenge Cup, arriving at Wigan North West railway station on a Sunday for the first time.

Supporters line the route for the 1965 Challenge Cup homecoming.

Wallgate is flooded with supporters waiting patiently for the Wigan bus to arrive.

1985
Wigan 28 Hull 24
Saturday May 4th

Final team: Ashby, Boston, Ashton, Holden, Lake, Hill, Parr, Gardiner, Clarke, McTigue, Stephens, Evans, Gilfedder.

Stephenson, Whitfield, Gill, Cannon, Stephens, Hemsley, Tamati, Case, West, Scott, Pendlebury. Subs: Elvin, Juliff.

It should have been the homecoming of all homecomings when Wigan ended a 20-year break from Challenge Cup winning tradition – even more so given they had been to Wembley and lost the previous year. But a downpour and a coach fuel leak at Newport Pagnell meant 20,000 fans had to wait an extra hour in the rain before the victorious team arrived. Even then many fans only saw the team arrive in the closed bus and saw Nicky Kiss and Henderson Gill holding the Cup in a steamed-up window. They switched to the open-top vehicle for the journey from Central Park to the Town Hall.

Vice-chairman Maurice Lindsay apologised to fans and revealed it

1984
Wigan 6 Widnes 19
Saturday May 5th

This is included here since the 1984 Challenge Cup campaign was the first evidence of Wigan's revival, and at least proved they could go all the way. The game and the homecoming are remembered most for the youthful Shaun Edwards – at 17 years, six months and 19 days he became the youngest ever player in a Challenge Cup Final and was Wigan's best player on the day.

Final team: Edwards, Ramsdale,

A tearful, 17-year-old Shaun Edwards received a hero's welcome when Wigan returned home empty-handed from Wembley in 1984. Coach Alex Murphy said: "He felt he'd let the side down. He hadn't of course – if anything it was the other way around."

The year the coach broke down – Wigan return to Central Park in 1985 and somewhere within that coach is the Challenge Cup. The fans had to wait an extra hour in the pouring rain – but it was worth it.

Fans would climb on to anything to get a good view of the victorious team and the Challenge Cup Trophy in 1985.

was one of the players that had helped them get home. He said: "Luckily Colin Whitfield is a trained diesel fitter. If he hadn't have been there we would never have got home at all."

In 1985 Wiganers found any vantage point for Wigan's first Wembley homecoming in 20 years. They clambered on to the hire shop roof to see the bus come up Riverway, turn into Hilton Street and stop on the forecourt.

Final team: Edwards, Ferguson, Stephenson, Donlan, Gill, Kenny, Ford, Courtney, Kiss, Case, West, Dunn, Potter. Subs: Du Toit, Campbell.

1988
Wigan 32 Halifax 12
Saturday April 30th

It wasn't the greatest of Finals, but the homecoming went off without a hitch. More than 30,000 crammed into Central Park on Sunday to see the side, skippered by Shaun Edwards, show off the famous trophy. "What great people," coach Graham Lowe said. "The people of Wigan live for their rugby league and this is why victory is so important to them." Maurice Lindsay had everyone reaching for their handkerchiefs when he said, "We have some tough guys in our team but they

The fans turned out in force for the 1988 homecoming. Little did they know they would be doing the same thing for the next seven years.

Nicky Kiss savours another Challenge Cup triumph for Wigan, this time in 1988. Kiss won the trophy with Wigan in 1985, 1988 and 1989.

have been touched by the reception given to them." The open-top bus made its way from the Central Park party to the Town Hall, a route lined with fans.

Final team: Lydon, T. Iro, K. Iro, Bell, Gill, Edwards, Gregory, Case, Kiss, Iford, Goodway, Potter, Hanley. Subs: Byrne, Wane.

1989
Wigan 27 St Helens 0
Saturday April 29th

Wigan were perhaps at their most lethal at Wembley this year, and it

For the second year running, Wigan return to Central Park with the Challenge Cup. Even the policeman wants a photograph.

was against the Old Enemy. The biggest of homecomings was

More Challenge Cup homecoming parties, this time 1989 – the poster proclaims one of Wigan's finest performances at Wembley.

guaranteed. 35,000 fans were at Central Park for one of the club's finest moments in its history and every player was cheered onto the podium at the ground. Coach Graham Lowe showed-off his musical talents by playing the guitar and fans climbed halfway up the floodlight towers – either to get a better view or escape the guitar playing! Supporters even brought their pets along and dressed them up in cherry and white garb. Of the eight homecomings in a row, many will remember this as the best.

Final team: Hampson, T. Iro, K. Iro, Bell, Lydon, Edwards, Gregory, Lucas, Kiss, Shelford, Platt, Potter, Hanley. Subs: Betts, Goodway.

1990
Wigan 36 Warrington 14
Saturday April 28th

By now Wiganers were familiar with the homecoming party, but new coach John Monie wasn't familiar with the Wembley lore. "It's just another working day," he told the *Wigan Observer*. For Shaun Edwards it was a nightmare. He suffered a double fracture to his cheekbone in a first-half clash and was still in hospital receiving treatment when his teammates paraded the trophy around Wigan on the Sunday. Central Park became a disco and Dean Bell, Kevin Iro and Adrian Shelford performed their war dance. The players' formal suits had been replaced by cherry and white tracksuits as the team and the town had more and more fun with the event.

Final team: Hampson, Lydon, Iro, Bell, Preston, Edwards, Gregory, Shelford, Dermott, Platt, Betts, Goodway, Hanley. Subs: Goulding, Gildart.

1991
Wigan 13 St Helens 8
Saturday April 27th

The open top bus rolls into Wigan for the fourth year in succession.

Another St Helens defeat at the Twin Towers meant another big party back in Wigan the day after when the team arrived home.

There were 18,000 inside Central Park and another 8,000 on the streets. Among the cabaret acts this year were Tom Jones's *It's Not Unusual* performed by Kevin Iro and Dean Bell, Martin Dermott gave us *Saturday Night At The Movies* with backing vocals from Frano Botica, Lance Todd Trophy winner Denis Betts sang *I Feel Good* while Andy Platt risked his life when he belted out *When The Saints Go Marching In*. Speaking of St Helens, at Knowsley Road barely 1,000 fans turned out to see the Saints third losers' homecoming in the last five years.

Final team: Hampson, Myers, Iro, Bell, Botica, Edwards, Gregory, Lucas, Dermott, Platt, Betts, Clarke, Hanley. Subs: Goulding, Goodway.

David Myers, Denis Betts and Frano Botica celebrate at Central Park in the 1991 homecoming.

The 1991 homecoming saw Wigan director Jack Robinson getting thrown in the bath by the players. Maurice Lindsay is worried that he might be next...

1992
Wigan 28 Castleford 12
Saturday May 2nd

Castleford were favourites to lose this one but bravely pointed out they had never been beaten at Wembley. Wigan put the record straight and the annual homecoming party was on again. More than 30,000 turned out in sunny weather and, with the smell of burgers

Martin Offiah is mobbed by Wigan supporters during the 1992 party.

"Ooh! This trophy's cold!" Billy McGinty, Denis Betts and Steve Hampson at the 1992 Wembley homecoming.

A familiar sight in Hilton Street as Wigan bring home the Challenge Cup again.

and chips in the air, the carnival started once more. As well as the sing-songs and the now standard playing of Tina Turner's *Simply The Best*, a new stunt was added to the homecoming repertoire. The players tried to walk the length of the goal-post crossbar in a test of nerves, balance, and how well they could take their alcohol. Denis Betts was the only one to make it across.

Final team: Lydon, Botica, Bell, Miles, Offiah, Edwards, Gregory, Skerrett, Dermott, Platt, Betts, McGinty, Clarke. Subs: Hampson, Cowie.

Wigan players strike a familiar pose atop the winners' bus as they head to Central Park for yet another homecoming party.

Outsiders Widnes gave Wigan an almighty scare, and Bobbie Goulding – who had by now defected to Widnes and played against Wigan at Wembley – ended the contest by sparking a brawl after landing a high tackle on Jason Robinson. Other than that it was business as usual. More than 20,000 fans packed Central Park and the streets were lined with fans as the bus drove in from Marus Bridge. The biggest cheer of the afternoon was reserved for departing coach John Monie. Martin Offiah explained the Wigan psychology behind the unprecedented winning streak. "The fear of losing is now perhaps a stronger spur than the adulation of winning."

Final team: Hampson, Robinson, Lydon, Farrar, Offiah, Botica, Edwards, Skerrett, Dermott, Platt, Betts, Clarke, Bell. Subs: Panapa, Farrell.

1994
Wigan 26 Leeds 16
Saturday April 30th

The fans leave Central Park after another happy Wembley homecoming, 1994.

Last year's homecoming party had doubled as a farewell bash for John Monie. This year it was John Dorahy's turn to wave goodbye to the Central Park throng. There was more tragic news for Denis Betts, whose mother died during the Final. Even though this was Wigan's seventh Wembley win in a row, the enthusiasm of the fans never diminished. T-shirts with the words: 'Wigan – Seventh Wonder of the World' became fashion items and Va'aiga Tuigamala had *The Clothes Show* researchers scrambling around in a panic when he came home sporting some colourful shirtwear.

Final team: Connolly, Tuigamala,

Dean Bell, Andy Platt, Paul Atcheson and a young-looking Andy Farrell celebrate their 1994 Challenge Cup Final win over Leeds. Behind them you can just see B. J. Mather and Sam Panapa.

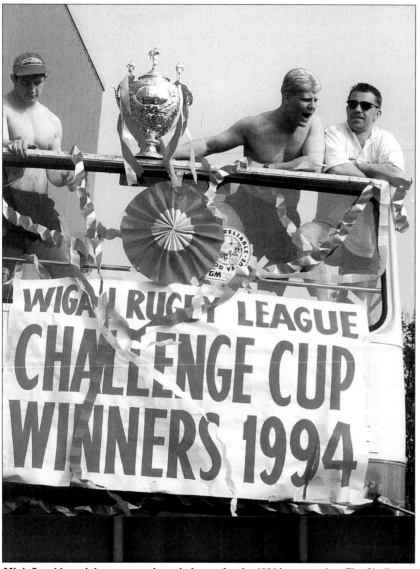

waved 'Eight In A Row' banners and bright sparks were already planning future slogans like 'Now it's Nine and Wigan's Fine' and 'A Decade of Dominance' for the year after. Wiganers had every right to be bullish about it. Phil Clarke won this year's Worst Singer Award in front of another packed Central Park. Sadly, of course, it would be the last time Central Park ever saw such a celebration.

Final team: Paul, Robinson, Tuigamala, Connolly, Offiah, Botica, Edwards, Skerrett, Hall, Cowie, Betts, Cassidy, Clarke. Subs: Farrell, Atcheson.

Mick Cassidy and the team work on their tans for the 1994 homecoming. The Challenge Cup has now been at Central Park seven years running – and Cass is not about to let go of the trophy here.

By 1995 even Henry Paul was struck down with 'Shirtless Homecoming Syndrome'. There is no sign of the fans' enthusiasm waning, though, as Paul shows-off Wigan's eighth Challenge Cup success in a row.

Bell, Mather, Offiah, Botica, Edwards, Skerrett, Dermott, Platt, Betts, Farrell, Clarke. Subs: Cassidy, Panapa.

1995
Wigan 30 Leeds 10
Saturday April 29th

The official reception was held at Central Park for the first time, and although the bus was late getting back the fans didn't care. Many

The one that got away. Wigan were such heavy favourites to beat Sheffield Eagles in the 1998 Challenge Cup Final it was almost inevitable they would lose! Even so, Warriors' supporters went to Central Park to welcome home their heroes.

Down by the Riverside

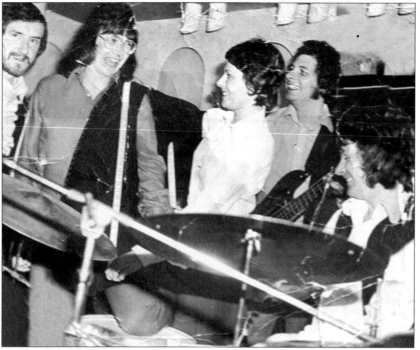

John Martin here with Mike Harvey guitarist, Dave Price on drums and Tim Peters the keyboard player. John's wife Barbara is fitting the band with their brand New Riverside Club suits.

IN THE SUMMER of 1966 a social club opened at Central Park at the Pavilion end of the ground. It was a good idea at the time but the club never really took off and it was only 10 years later when it was re-named The Riverside that the nightspot became a venue in its own right, rather than just another room at Central Park.

Whether the original board of directors intended hen parties to be dancing on chairs to The Drifters, or envisaged male strip shows enthralling the mainly female audience, is a matter of debate. What is not in question is that The Riverside Club survived the 'disco era' where the more famous Wigan Casino failed. While Wigan Rugby Club did it on the field, The Riverside Club did it on the chairs!

In September 1976, John Martin was compering at Fagin's nightclub in Manchester. One afternoon he had two customers, Ian Clift and Tom Bennett, directors of Wigan rugby league club, who had a proposition for him.

Martin said: "They invited me over for a drink. They said they had a club in Wigan and asked if I would be interested in managing it. They arranged a meeting with me at the club, and what a shock to the system that was.

"It was a Sunday afternoon. I opened the door and saw these six gigantic windows overlooking the

An early practice session at The Riverside Club.

car park, there was oil cloth on the floor and the place smelled of floor cleaner. There were only kids in. We went behind the bar where the committee were sorting out their finances, rolling out the tenners, which didn't seem to be right thing to do.

"In the end someone must have tipped Fagin's off because they learned that I had been over to Wigan. It meant that I had little choice but to make the move."

Under pressure to move or not, Martin brought adults back into the newly-named Riverside Club and got the venue back on its feet. For the first time it got a reputation as a place to go. Quality acts were booked and the room was smartened up to give it more of a club feel. New carpets were put in, curtains were put over the windows and the chairs were painted. Martin ran the club for four years and built up its image, and by 1980 The Riverside Club was a bigger success than the rugby club – which was about to be relegated.

Recognising the success of The Riverside, Wigan brought in Wigan Casino owner Jerry Marshall to oversee proceedings. According to Martin a deal was struck behind his back and by 1986 he decided to leave The Riverside Club. "Jerry could see the business was doing well and he asked me to stay on as manager," Martin said. "I did until 1986 but I wasn't getting anywhere so I left and went to Blighty's in Farnworth.

"The Riverside was bouncing when I left it but within six months they were getting eight people in on Friday and even less on Saturday."

Wigan asked Martin to come back and he did, but his brief six-month spell in Farnworth was to

The original poster for The Riverside Club. How could anyone resist?

A star is born! Long before anyone had even dreamed of the Riverside Club – assuming anyone ever did dream of the Riverside Club – John Martin was packing them in at Sheffield.

spark a famous tradition at The Riverside. It was at Blighty's where the idea of dancing on chairs first materialised.

"We came across that by acci-

dent," Martin recalled. "There was a party in there one night, and I suppose you could say they were a bit over-zealous. They got up on the chairs and started dancing, and

John Martin with Henry Cooper at The Riverside Club – note the subtle bow ties.

before we knew it everyone had followed. But the atmosphere was unbelievable.

"When I came back to The Riverside we got some steel chairs in. We had a welding company make one up for us and we liked what we saw. So that's what we did – we filled the place with steel chairs.

"People got the idea pretty quickly. There are some that say they'll never get up but give them a while and they're up. Next thing you know you can't get them down. At some places if you got up on a chair the bouncers would throw you out in next to no time. At the Riverside if you didn't get up on a chair we put the spotlight on you and shouted, 'You're a boring b******!'"

All the well-known acts have performed at The Riverside. Comedians Bernard Manning and Roy 'Chubby' Brown, Bob Monkhouse and Ken Dodd have all done their stuff there, and far too many bands to name.

The Riverside's audience was predominantly female, and that was deliberate. The majority of those that went were large parties and the percentage of men that made up the throng was restricted. Groups from Haydock Races were popular, but hen nights were the Riverside Club's speciality "When they're on a hen night they don't want men harassing them," Martin explained. "They just want a drink, a good time. They are not strolling round a disco, trying to get picked up. So we kept audiences mostly female. It worked well that way.

"I would say that only 15 or 20 per cent of the audience were from Wigan. The rest came from other areas, and more than 75 per cent were coach parties."

Martin, originally from Oldham, worked in the Channel Islands for a while before he returned to the club scene in Manchester. The Riverside, though, has been his pride and joy. "I've enjoyed my working life and there aren't many people who can say that. The Riverside has been very kind to me and I wouldn't have changed anything."

While there was plenty of fun in full view of the paying customer, there was also some fun behind the scenes, too. There was, for instance, a time when the head barman inadvertently blew up the dressing room after mistaking a tin of fireworks' gunpowder for an ashtray, and other stories too lurid for a re-telling here.

One tale worth telling dates back to some of the first Christmas parties at the club, one where Martin was entertainer and chef all in one. More used to the stage, Martin arrived for work at 7.30 in the evening convinced he would have no problem cooking for 120, only to realise very quickly that it WAS going to be problem.

"They were supposed to be eating at eight o'clock," Martin recalled. "I think it was about 10.30pm when we finished serving – or so we thought. One of the girls came in and said, 'The Hunter party hasn't had anything yet!' There was a bit of a panic, but nothing compared to the state we got in when we realised we had run out of turkey.

"So I decided to defrost some pre-cooked chicken and we gave them that. When the guy came to pay his bill later he said, 'Thanks for a great night, but tell me, do you have a problem with your turkey?'"

The final anecdote is not for the squeamish. "The ladies toilets were always blocking up," Martin explained. "This one night we thought the pipes had frozen up outside and myself and the manager, Phil Taylor, went to see if we could sort it out."

Wearing dinner jackets and using blow lamps in the dark, the two located the offending pipe outside the building. At one corner there was a rodding hole, and Taylor, standing at the top of a ladder to reach it, had the bright idea of opening up the valve with a spanner. Pressure caused the contents of the pipe to fly out, and the manager, with nowhere to go, took it all in the face.

They may get close to emulating the atmosphere of The Riverside Club at the JJB Sports Stadium. But they'll never get to tell tales like that again.

Central Park ... Sold

AS FAR BACK as 1995, Wigan Rugby League club was looking at the possibility of leaving Central Park and sharing a new stadium with Wigan Athletic.

Talks went on for six months between both clubs and Wigan Borough Council, when the Robin Park site was being considered for a 25,000-seat stadium, but the discussions broke down in November 1996. By that time, Wigan's Challenge Cup and league championship crowns had both gone, attendances were falling, players were being sold to cut costs, and there was even more turmoil off the field. Something had to give – and it did.

The beginning of the end of Central Park came at The Willows on Sunday February 11th 1996. After winning the Challenge Cup for eight successive years, Wigan had already despatched Bramley by a record 74-12 in the fourth round and faced Salford in the next.

With confidence sky-high, the Wigan players were granted a week-off prior to the game and some took advantage to go on holiday to Tenerife. Whether that or sheer arrogance led to their 26-16 defeat, no one could have foreseen the huge repercussions of that shock result.

First, it cost the club £300,000 just by not getting to the Final – let alone winning it – a sum of money the management appeared to have counted on getting. For several years Wigan had spent a large part of their winnings buying and paying the best players, effectively working on a 'break-even' basis. So after gate receipts started to fall as Wigan's dominance led to complacency with the fans, and then the club failed to win the Challenge Cup and the league – now Super League – in 1996, finances were being stretched.

The club arranged two cross-code games with Bath to try and raise more cash, but it also saw another way to make money – one which would end with chairman Jack Robinson appearing in court.

The *Wigan Observer* criticised the club for allowing its players a week off before the Salford game, but made the mistake of including Neil Cowie in the players that went partying in Tenerife. Cowie, in fact, was on holiday in Scotland, and solicitors acting for both Wigan and Cowie contacted the paper, demanding an apology.

The club also threatened to sue for libel, claiming that Cowie was involved in a £150,000 transfer deal with Leeds, and that the paper's inaccurate allegations had caused

that deal to fall through. But in a subsequent court hearing it was said such a deal never existed.

Believing this, the *Wigan Observer* informed the police and they subsequently arrested Robinson, Wigan director and Cowie's father-in-law John Martin, and Cowie himself. Cowie and Martin were released without charge, but Robinson appeared before Bolton Crown Court in March 1997 on three charges, including intent to pervert the cause of justice. The jury found Robinson not guilty on all three charges.

Even while the court proceedings were grinding on, there was more trouble back at Central Park. With rugby union now a professional sport there was some silly money flying around, and Wigan had to fight to keep its players. However, one way of raising money was by selling players. Between the 1996 and 1997 seasons, Wigan began cost-cutting with the sales of Joe Lydon, Shaun Edwards, Martin Offiah and Va'aiga Tuigamala, as well as losing coach Graeme West, but this created a snowball effect. Wigan consequently continued to lose more games and fans, and once again, in 1997, went out of the Challenge Cup at an early stage – against arch-rivals St Helens.

This is how Central Park might have looked had Dave Whelan's proposals to develop the stadium gone through.

On January 11th 1997, two months after talks between Wigan Athletic and Wigan Borough Council about a Robin Park joint stadium had broken down, shareholders met to discuss the future of Central Park. Robinson saw its prime location as a means of making money, if the ground could be sold, and he saw that as a necessary step in having a new stadium in the borough, one that could have raised more revenue through corporate hospitality. Tesco had offered to buy the ground for £12m, and Wigan could play at Bolton's new Reebok stadium in Horwich while a new stadium was

Wigan chairman Jack Robinson, directors and mystery men leave the Oak Hotel in February. The Tesco deal goes ahead.

How Tesco's envisage what the site will look like when work on their new superstore is complete.

built. But JJB boss Dave Whelan also saw his opportunity, having already taken over Wigan Athletic, and he proposed to buy Central Park for £4m and spend £11m redeveloping it – in return for receiving 10 per cent of the gate receipts.

Shareholders voted in favour of the Whelan proposal by 7-1, yet Robinson and vice-chairman Tom Rathbone sold the ground to Tesco.

There was nothing anyone could do, since their debenture shares meant they effectively had total control of the club anyway. Martin resigned in February, claiming the deal had been without his knowledge, and Whelan, angered that his proposal had been voted on and yet ignored, pressed ahead with plans for a new stadium for Wigan Athletic at Robin Park, and severed all contacts with Wigan Warriors.

The club called an extraordinary general meeting on April 10th, where it explained it had been forced into a quick sale because

Martin had demanded his £240,000 stake in the club following his resignation. But negotiations were already under way with Tesco and Bolton before Martin

John Martin explains why he left the board of directors in February 1997. "They went ahead and made the decision without telling anyone," he said at the time.

resigned. Martin was also willing to defer the payment of his stake in the club if a meeting of shareholders had been called to consider a resolution on the proposed sale to

Tesco, but no such resolution was brought.

The fact that talks had taken place about selling Central Park and moving to Bolton before Martin resigned came to light through a leaked letter, which went further than suggesting Wigan took up temporary residence at the Reebok stadium. Addressed to Bolton's board of directors, the letter said playing rugby at Horwich was 'an exciting and forward-thinking prospect'. It went on to say: 'We would like to look closely at a longer term relationship, whereby the costs and profits of such an arrangement are shared equitably between the two clubs.'

Now many fans were incensed and as well as falling attendances, Wigan had noisy supporter demonstrations to contend with. Supporters and shareholders groups were formed as people got their heads together to think of some way of preventing the deal. By the middle of March a shareholder called Ernie Benbow, who

Ernie Benbow, who campaigned throughout 1997 for changes at the top and a re-think on how power was distributed throughout the shareholders. The latter point is academic now.

A protest from supporters at Central Park in 1997. Many supporters protested simply by staying away.

Protesters against the board of directors hand out leaflets prior to a game at Central Park.

In the Shareholders Action Group camp, Ernie Benbow and Tom Arkwright outline what the shareholders can and can't do – meeting here at Wigan Cricket Club.

Legally, the shareholders were entitled to call an extraordinary meeting and they did just that. Here Ernie Benbow serves the requisition on the club.

worked as an NHS trust manager, used the club's company rules to call an extraordinary general meeting with resolutions to remove Robinson and Rathbone from the board, as well as repay the debenture stock, which would remove the directors' overall controlling rights over the club.

A battle for support began. The EGM had been called for May 20th and as the weeks rolled by,

Wigan's commercial manager David Bradshaw and club solicitor face the media in 1997.

Members of the Shareholders Action Group, fighting to have the chairman and vice-chairman removed from the board, hand in proxy votes at Central Park in the run-up to the confidence vote on May 20th 1997.

Wigan fans sign a petition to save Central Park, but by this time the ground was already sold. Even the dog wants to stay!

Chairman Jack Robinson and vice-chairman Tom Rathbone celebrate after surviving a confidence vote at Central Park on May 20th 1997. Their joy would be shortlived.

Robinson went about canvassing for support. When the big night came, both Robinson and Rathbone survived by 80 votes, and the debenture stock remained intact by virtue of 12 votes. In each case a show of hands was deemed too close to call.

As fortunes on the field plunged in 1996 and 1997, and the row behind the scenes as to the club's future went on, attendances at Central Park dropped alarmingly.

At a meeting in the Oak Hotel, relatives of people whose ashes were scattered on the Central Park pitch met to discuss what they could do to prevent the turf being ripped up without any consideration. Among those whose ashes are on the ground are Jim Sullivan and Tom Bradshaw.

After allegations of vote-rigging emerged from the May 20th extraordinary general meeting, Ernie Benbow and solicitor Peter Norbury took their evidence to Wigan Police Station in June 1997.

Jack Robinson and Tom Rathbone in their usual seats at Central Park watching Wigan take on Leeds. In 1997 they were forced to leave them as the financial crisis at the club came to a head.

Supporters against the sale of Central Park took their protests to the Town Hall, where planning permission would be granted...

After the meeting came allegations of vote-rigging. Robinson's opponents claimed votes had not been filled in properly, and that some had been 'manufactured'. In July a retired miner made a sworn statement to say the club had asked him to canvass shareholders in the Westhoughton area. He was asked to get the shareholders to sign the proxy vote form but leave out the name of the person they were appointing to vote in their place.

It was also discovered that more than 160 names had been removed from the club's 1996 shareholder register and that by June 1997 nearly 180 had been added, many of these employees at the club and their relatives and friends. It became apparent that enough shares could have changed hands prior to the meeting in May to have influenced the outcome of the three issues voted upon. The club had used the powers in its company rules to carry out the transfers, though questions remained as to whether all the rules had been complied with in every case.

It is still not clear why Robinson

...and to the Tesco headquarters in Hertfordshire.

They even went to the Reebok Stadium in Horwich after the club had been in discussions with Bolton Wanderers about sharing their new ground with Wigan.

And still the protests went on at Central Park while reults on the field continued to suffer.

One of the youngest 'Save Central Park' campaigners was Chloe Brooks, of Garswood, seen here at the age of five months. She will probably never remember what it was like at Central Park.

they resigned surely played a part. There was no money to pay the bill, players' wages had been delayed for the previous two months, and the NatWest Bank refused to advance Wigan £1m, against what was thought to be an

John Martin resigned as a director in February 1997 in protest against the other board members. Here he gives his reaction to the resignations of Jack Robinson and Tom Rathbone, outside Central Park, in August that year.

agreed £1.5m, while both Robinson and Rathbone remained in office. Despite winning through a confidence vote in May, the pressure became too much.

Director Arthur Thomas took over as acting chairman, but when and Rathbone resigned when they did. Rathbone went on August 19th and Robinson followed him the day after. A police inquiry into the vote-rigging allegations and a £200,000 tax bill due a day before he left in October the decks had effectively been cleared. Whelan, who had refused to deal with the club while the old board of directors was in charge, now pressed ahead with plans to allow Wigan to play at the new stadium at Robin Park. A new chairman was appointed, auditors came in to study the books, and it was revealed that the club owed a total of £6m.

In essence, Wigan lost Central Park because, during its years of unprecedented success during the early 1990s, the club was spending as much as it was winning. A financial report compiled by Ernst and Young stated that: 'A major reason for the current financial problems is that Wigan Football Club have operated in the past close to a break even situation at a period of maximum success with little scope for managing any downturn.'

They estimated the loss to the year ending May 1996 at £738,000, and believed that the truncated season from August 1995 to January 1996, when there were only 10 home games compared to 15 the previous season, had a big effect. Attendances were down, and the club paid one-off loyalty bonuses to players in August 1995 totalling £225,000 in a bid to keep them in the new Super League.

As the debts mounted, it was clear that one way to reverse the trend would be to sell off assets, including the ground and players. When that was not enough, those who had sold the ground had nowhere else to turn, and by now the fans – the lifeblood of any sports club, were largely against them.

After new faces had been appointed at the top there were more developments to come, but Central Park's fate had already been decided. Planning permission was granted and the timetable was set so that development work on Tesco's new supermarket should have started by December 1999. The club had already received a deposit of £1.5m and was to receive further money under the sale in November 1999, two months after the last rugby match played at the ground.

When Dave Whelan took over the club in March 1998 and secured its financial future, after shareholders agreed to sell their holdings to him, Wigan's move to Robin Park was also secured. Supporters fought on to save Central Park, but at least the club now had a new home to go to.

In recommending the deal, the then club chairman Mike Nolan said: "It is difficult to see any viable

Sportswear millionaire Dave Whelan took an interest in Wigan rugby club when its money-spinning power appeared to slip in the early 1990s. The Wigan board of directors did not want to let him in, though, as they feared he would take over. Eventually, Whelan had to step in as there appeared to be no other way to reverse the club's fortunes.

Dave Whelan unveils his plans for a new stadium at Robin Park, pictured here with Wigan Borough Council leader Peter Smith.

alternative, either to meet the short term financial needs of the club, or, more importantly, to take the club forward."

At the meeting in March 1998, when shareholders cleared the way for the purchase to go ahead, they too admitted there was no other way out. Wigan had enjoyed years of success, but at the cost of their famous home ground.

Following that meeting only two seasons remained at Central Park. The team made the most of the first, getting to the Challenge Cup Final and winning the Inaugural Grand Final later in the year. After that success interest in the club sky-rocketed and it sold thousands of season tickets, with fans wanting to play a part in the last Central Park year. The 1999 Super League was the longest yet with 15 home games, and that would please fans who loved the ground. But Super League went further still to ensure the last home game was special by pitting Wigan against St Helens.

Wigan's New Home

WIGAN Rugby League has entered a whole new era. They have a new name, and now they have a new home.

The JJB Sports Stadium makes Central Park look puny in comparison. It is bigger in every dimension, grander in design, and far more dominant over its immediate surroundings. Yet in terms of memories, in terms of what it means to different people, in terms of being a landmark, the only landmark, that instantly identifies the town of Wigan, it is the new structure that is puny. It will take at least half a century and teams of unparalleled success before the JJB Sports Stadium can be as revered as the drafty terraces on Joe Hill's field. And even then, Central Park will not be forgotten.

Nostalgia should not be allowed to halt progress. Central Park is all about nostalgia and the town's heritage, for the structure itself has no significance. The original pavilion building has been swallowed up by metal cladding, the pavilion end unrecognisable from the days before the social club was built, where a row of turnstiles once stood. The final Douglas Stand was built in the 1970s, and only the Kop end and the Popular Side

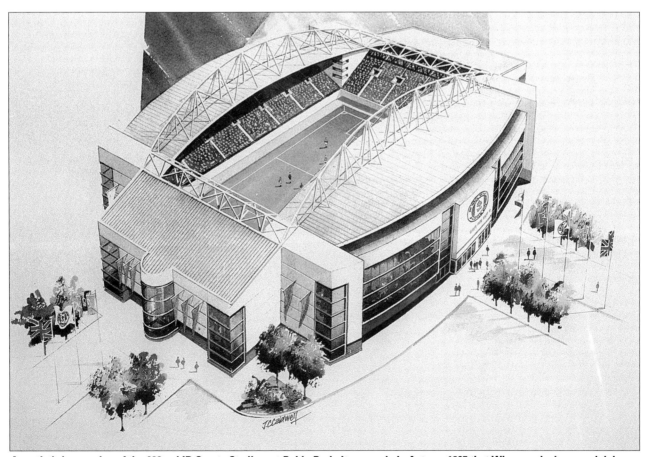

An artist's impression of the £28m JJB Sports Stadium at Robin Park. It was only in Autumn 1997 that Wigan rugby league club knew their future was safe there.

Will the ground bring as much good fortune as Central Park has to Wigan rugby league?

remain similar to their original designs. Different people have their own memories of how Central Park used to be, marked in time by the great players who graced the turf. It is impossible to preserve them all.

So the club has moved on, and while all those associated with it, from the players to the supporters, will look back at the Central Park times for years to come, they hope it will not be long before Wigan has a new breed of sporting heroes, and more sweeping success.

Only then will the new era well and truly dawn.

When planning permission for a new 25,000 all-seater stadium was given by Wigan Borough Council in 1997, Wigan Athletic looked as though they might have the whole thing for themselves. But when Dave Whelan, the man financing the project, gained majority share-

holder control of Wigan Warriors in 1998, the groundsharing idea that had been discussed between Wigan Athletic, Wigan RL and the Council back in 1995 became a reality.

In little over a year the £28m structure was built, changing the Wigan skyline forever and re-drawing the town centre map. Springfield Park and Central Park have gone, and the area known as Robin Park – an expanse of playing fields just four years ago – has become a modern-day mecca for athletes of all sporting persuasions.

Wigan Warriors will play all their home matches at the JJB Stadium, as will Wigan Athletic. Neither club will be able to claim that the stadium is their own, and it is inevitable that the single

The JJB Stadium, built by Alfred McAlpine plc – the new home of Wigan Warriors.

ground will bring both clubs and their respective supporters closer together.

There are four stands, which at the time of writing were only named after the compass point at which they lined the pitch. The North and South stands, at the goal ends, each have 5,400 seats. The East stand houses the biggest number of spectators with 8,178 seats, while the West stand opposite, housing the media and directors, executive boxes, and cut through with the players' tunnel, has 6,022 seats.

The pitch, bigger than Central Park's, measures 110 metres by 60 metres and is made up of a combination of natural grass and man-made fibres which, it is hoped, will cope with 12 months' continuous use for rugby and football. The first seeds were sown in September 1998.

The players' changing rooms are on the ground floor of the West Stand and provide everything the sportsman needs. As well as showers and baths, there is a doctor's room, a nasty-sounding 'stitching' room, physio room and even a drugs testing room. As well as the two main changing rooms there are smaller, separate rooms for reserve teams.

All travelling fans are housed in the North stand. Concourses built on a first-floor level have all the eating booths, refreshments and toilets, and all the seats accessed from this level. The disabled have designated platforms and their own specially-adapted facilities.

The main ticket office is in the north-west corner of the stadium, facing towards Anjou Boulevard where the cinema, nightclub, restaurant and bingo hall is located. There are automated ticket machines as well as manned counters. Two new roads and 2,500 car parking spaces have been created to serve the ground.

In total, the stadium has cost £28 million to build. Central Park cost £500.

In 1902, the *Wigan Examiner* stated: 'The enclosure, which henceforth will be known as Central Park, is one of the best equipped grounds in the county.'

In 1997, the *Wigan Observer* said: 'Wigan Warriors will play the first rugby league of the next millennium at the JJB Stadium, one of the best grounds in the country.'

The first chapter in the history of Wigan rugby league is complete.

A new one has begun.

Subscribers

James Abbott
Bill Abernethey
Barry Abernethy
Tony Ackroyd
James Ainscough
Vincent Alker
All The Patients at Wigan & Leigh Hospice
Anthony Allcock
Gordon Allen
Donald Armstrong
Neil Armstrong
Dean Elton Arstall
Frank James Ashcroft
Victor A Ashcroft
Dr Zoe Ashley
Richard Ashton
John Barrie Ashurst
Roy Ashurst
Mr Alfred Aspinall
Ray Atherton

David Baggeley
Mary Banks
Alan H Barker
Philip Geoffrey Barker
Mark Barlow
Simon Barlow
Gordon Baron
Neal W Baron
Dave Bartlett (Euxton)
Daniel Barton
Mr Malcolm Barton
Mr Spencer Barton
Susan & Michael Basnett
Peter Battersby
Alice Beaton
John Benn
Mr Ray Bent
Alaine Berry
Mr B Berry
Bob Berry
David Berry

Neil Berry
Gordon E Bibby
Joe Bilsborough
John Bilsborough
Harold Birch
E G Boardman
Anthony-Glen Boffey
Jim Bolton
Stephen H Bond
Jim Bould
David Boydell
Sarah Boydell
Peter John Boyle
Ken Bradley
Marlene Bradley
Roy Bradley
Mr Graham Bradshaw
Bernard Brady
Mr David Brennan
Jim Brennan
John Joseph Brewder
Ann Brogan
Brenda Brown
Mr Cliff Brown
William Brown
Derek Buckley
Andy Bulman
John Burke, Ex-Wigan RL
G W Burns
Tommy Burns
Mr Paul Burton

Neil Cain
William Robert Caldwell
Peter & Lynne Carroll
Dennis R Carter
Ernest Steven and Dean Cartwright
Mr Peter Carty
Stanley Brian Causey
Chris Chamberlain
Jon Chamberlain
A & M E Chambers

Derek Chapman
Keith Cherrington
Mrs Joyce H Churchill
David and Marguerite Clark
Jeffrey James Clark
Frank Clayton
Clegg Family
Dez Coley
Arthur Collier
Mr Robert Collier
Alan Cooper
Sue Cooper
Mr Ralph Cornish
Maurice Cox
Mr F Crank
Philip Croasdale
Julia & Keith Crook
Leslie Crook
Neil Crook
David Joseph Croston
Dr J B Crummett
John Crumpton
Derrick Cunliffe
Leslie Cunliffe
Percy Cunliffe

Edward George Stephen Dainty
Paul Dainty
Brian & Jonathan Dale
Mary Dale
Paul Danbury
James Darbyshire
John Davenport
Alf Davis
Mr Harvey Davis
Barry Dawber
James Dawber
Brian Dean
David Dean Snr
John Dean
Ken Deluce
Jack Dean Denton
Mr Denis Dermott
Terence Dickinson
Mr Tom Dickinson
John Dillon
Ian Dixon
John Doyle

Cameron Don Duncan

James Eatock
John Eckersley
Mr Jack Edwards
John S Edwards
Simon Edwardson
Harry Howard Elce
James Norman Evans
S Evans, York RL Historian
Sam Evans
Mr William Evans

Francis David Fairhurst
Jack Fairhurst
Michael Fairhurst
Craig Fanning
Keith W Fanning
Malcolm Ferguson
Graham Fillingham
Geoffrey Finney
Michael Fishwick
Mr L Foster
Mr Malcolm Foster
Alan Fox
Ron Frampton
Neil Furby

Mike Gannon
Robert Gardner
Paul Antony Gaskell
Raymond Gaskell
Michael R Gill
Martin Gleeson
Derek Glover
Ian C Glover
Dr's M A & A M Glover
Stan Gostellow
Mrs Margaret Grant
Gillian Gray, Editor *Wigan Observer*
Miss B Sturgeon-Green
Colin Green
Denis W Green
Derek James Green
William Greenwood
Ronald Gregory
Colin Grey
Brian Griffin

Michelle P Hall
Eunice Hammond
Michael James Hannon
Kevin Hansen
Karl Hatherley
John Haydock
Keith Hayton
Mr Alan Hazard
Mr Ian Heads
Paul Heaton
Sarah Louise Heaton
Richard Henson
Antony Heyes
Stephen James Heyes
William Heyes
Winston Heyes
Eric Heywood
Alan Hickey
S M Higham
Billy Highton
Dave Hill
Norman Hilton
Donald H Hindley
John Hitchen
Joseph John Hitchen
Mr Kenneth Hodgkiss
Mr Bernard Hogan
James Holcroft
Robert E Holcroft
Mr Ronald Holland
Andy Hosking
Mr Alan Houghton
Brian Houghton
Steve Houghton
Edward Howard
Ken Howarth
Brian Hughes BSc
Malcolm Hulatt
Walter Hulatt
Alan Hunt
David and Susan Huntington
Derek Huntington
Andrew Hurst
Florence Hurst
Graham John Hurst
Jack Hurst
Joe Hutchinson

Clifford James
Peter Johnson (Whitley Bay)
Robert Johnson
Billy Jones
Susan E Jones

Mel Kennedy
Martin Kenrick
James John Kenyon
Janet Kenyon
Michael Killeen
Edward James Garforth King
Thomas Stephen King
Trevor Kinsley

Stephen Latham
Janet Lees
Warren Scott Leonard
Charles Lewis
David Gerald Lewis
Christopher Leyland
Mr George Leyland
Joe Lloyd
James A Lomax
Mr G A Lowe
Irene Lowe
Joe Lowe
John Lowe
Kenneth Lucas

David Maddocks
John A Maiden
David C Makin
Bernard Malley
Hilary Mangnall
Alan J Mark
Mr Stephen Marle
Francis and Christine Marron
Alice Joan Marshall
Tony Marshall
V F Marshall
Mrs E J Mason
John David Mason
Ronald Mather
Susan J Mather
William Mather
Paul "Canny" McCann
A J McCracken

W McCracken
S W McCracken
Jack McGirl
Mr Brian McGuire
Mr G F McGuire
Christopher B McHale
Stan McLeod (Ex Player 1961-64)
Gerard McLoughlin
Chris McVeigh
Norman Meadows
Andrew J Measey
Alfred Melling
Elizebeth Melling
Stan Melling
Tom Mills
Brett Mitchell
William Moffatt
Peter A Moir
Ben Molyneux
Glenn Moore
Anthony Moore
Robert Moore
Keith Wm Moorfield
Rob Moroney
Edith Molyneux Morris
Mr F Morris
Carl L Moss
Harold Moss
Michael Moss
Paul A Moss
Jim and June Moyers
Paul and Sharon Moyers
Carole Ann Moyle
Brian Murphy
Shaun Barrie Muscroft
James Myler

Steven John Naylor
John Harris Newton
John Matthew Nolan
Gilbert Norman

Peter O'Brien
Derek O'Mara
Steven Oddie
Carl Ormshaw
Dave Orrell

John Nigel Parkinson
Terence Parkinson
Joseph Parr
Gareth Parry (Salford)
Richard Parry
Mark Pattinson
Christine Paxton
Brian Pendlebury
Cyril Pendlebury
Jack Pendlebury
Mr Keith S Pendlebury
Michelle L Pennington
David Perry
Clifford Joseph Peters
Ernest Petrie
John Pimblett
Michael and Jane Pimblett
David Price
Kevin Priest
George Priestley
David Prince
William Prince
Derek Prior

Paul Raftery
Lynn White-Rampling
Paul Ratchford
Mrs Esther Rees
Alan Richardson
Bill Rigby
David A Rigby
David Alan Rigby
Mr Graham Rigby
Mr Harry Rigby
K Rigby
Maurice Rigby (Deceased)
Tony Rigby
Bill Riley, Wires Number One
Joe Riley
John Riley
M W E Roberts
Sue Robinson
John Rodden
Matthew & Philip Rogers
Paul Rogers
Allan Rogerson
Gareth Rook
Alan Rooney

Mr Brian Rostron
Alan Roughley
Robert Rourke
Mr L Russon
Mollie Ryding

Verity Sankey
D M W Santus
Tom Santus
Richard William Sawyer
Anthony Scally
H Scrivens
David Sear
Amanda Seddon
David J Seddon
Philip Seddon
Roy D Seddon
Tom Seddon
Christopher T Settle
Gerard Francis Shannon
Tom Sharples
Mr Graham Shaw
John Shaw
Maureen Shenton
Eric Silcock
Mr Alan Simms
Rita Skepp
Andrew Skett
Denis Skett
Stuwart Skett
Glen Sladen
Roy Smales
Nigel Smallshaw
Albert Smith
Colin Smith
David Smith
Jeffrey Smith
Nigel P Smith
Wayne A Smith
Tony Southworth
Denis Speakman
Roy Spear
Jon Spriggs
Graham Standish
Jason Stanton
Matthew Stanton
Richard Stanton
Mr Frederick Stewart

Charles Storey
David Sudworth
Keith R Sutch
John Mark Sutton
Shaun Sweeney

Alan P Taberner
Jim Taberner
Lester Taberner
Carol Talbot
Peter Talbot
Mr Brian Taylor
Giles M Taylor
Ian & Sharon Taylor
John Taylor
Bert Thompson
Paul Stephen Thompson
Arthur J Tice
Simon L Tollet
Anne Agnes Topping
Mrs Hnazant Toward
Stephen Trafford
Mike Trevena
Clifford Turner
Dave Turner
David H Turner
Michael Turner
John Twiss

Kenneth T Vale
Eunice Veasey
Richard Vincent
Stella L Vincent
Jonathan Vose

Mick Waldron
Gordon Walls
Len Walls
Mrs Doreen Walsh
Mr L Walton
Richard Norman Wardle
Keith Wareing
Adrian Watson
Bill and June Watts
Louetta Webb
David Welsh
Dropgoal Welshy
John Whelan

Michael Whelan
John M White
Samual Whittle
Ernest Mikel Wilby
Joseph Wilkinson
Barrie Williams
Leslie Williams
William Willis
Sharon T Wilmot
Brian Winnard
Geoff Winnard
William Wood
John Woods
Mr John Woolley
Mr & Mrs John Worthington
Christopher Wright
Jerry Wright
T G R Wright